Bison

Bison

The Yacc-compatible Parser Generator
September 2003, Bison Version 1.875, Eighth Edition

by Charles Donnelly and Richard Stallman

This manual was last updated September 2003 for GNU Bison (version 1.875), the GNU parser generator.

Published by:
GNU Press
a division of the
Free Software Foundation
59 Temple Place Suite 330
Boston, MA 02111-1307 USA

Website: www.gnupress.org
General: press@gnu.org
Orders: sales@gnu.org
Tel 617-542-5942
Fax 617-542-2652

ISBN 1-882114-23-X

Cover art by Etienne Suvasa. Cover design by Jonathan Richard.

Table of Contents

Introduction

Bison is a general-purpose parser generator that converts a grammar description for an LALR(1) context-free grammar into a C program to parse that grammar. Once you are proficient with Bison, you may use it to develop a wide range of language parsers, from those used in simple desk calculators to complex programming languages.

Bison is upward compatible with Yacc: all properly written Yacc grammars ought to work with Bison with no change. Anyone familiar with Yacc should be able to use Bison with little trouble. You need to be fluent in C programming in order to use Bison or to understand this manual.

We begin with tutorial chapters that explain the basic concepts of using Bison and give three explained examples, each building on the one before it. If you don't know Bison or Yacc, start by reading these chapters. Reference chapters follow which describe specific aspects of Bison in detail.

Bison was written primarily by Robert Corbett; Richard Stallman made it Yacc-compatible. Wilfred Hansen of Carnegie Mellon University added multicharacter string literals and other features.

This edition corresponds to version 1.875 of Bison.

Conditions for Using Bison

As of Bison version 1.24, we have changed the distribution terms for `yyparse` to permit using Bison's output in nonfree programs when Bison is generating C code for LALR(1) parsers. Formerly these parsers could be used only in programs that were free software.

The other GNU programming tools, such as the GNU C compiler, have never had such a requirement. They could always be used for nonfree software. The reason Bison was different was not due to a special policy decision; it resulted from applying the usual General Public License to all the Bison source code.

The output of the Bison utility—the Bison parser file—contains a verbatim copy of a sizable piece of Bison, which is the code for the `yyparse` function. (The actions from your grammar are inserted into this function at one point, but the rest of the function is not changed.) When we applied the GPL terms to the code for `yyparse`, the effect was to restrict the use of Bison output to free software.

We didn't change the terms because of sympathy for people who want to make software proprietary. **Software should be free.** But we concluded that limiting Bison's use to free software was doing little to encourage people to make other software free. So we decided to make the practical conditions for using Bison match the practical conditions for using the other GNU tools.

This exception applies only when Bison is generating C code for a LALR(1) parser; otherwise, the GPL terms operate as usual. You can tell whether the exception applies to your '.c' output file by inspecting it to see whether it says "As a special exception, when this file is copied by Bison into a Bison output file, you may use that output file without restriction."

GNU GENERAL PUBLIC LICENSE

Version 2, June 1991

Copyright © 1989, 1991 Free Software Foundation, Inc.
59 Temple Place - Suite 330, Boston, MA 02111-1307, USA

Everyone is permitted to copy and distribute verbatim copies
of this license document, but changing it is not allowed.

Preamble

The licenses for most software are designed to take away your freedom to share and change it. By contrast, the GNU General Public License is intended to guarantee your freedom to share and change free software—to make sure the software is free for all its users. This General Public License applies to most of the Free Software Foundation's software and to any other program whose authors commit to using it. (Some other Free Software Foundation software is covered by the GNU Library General Public License instead.) You can apply it to your programs, too.

When we speak of free software, we are referring to freedom, not price. Our General Public Licenses are designed to make sure that you have the freedom to distribute copies of free software (and charge for this service if you wish), that you receive source code or can get it if you want it, that you can change the software or use pieces of it in new free programs; and that you know you can do these things.

To protect your rights, we need to make restrictions that forbid anyone to deny you these rights or to ask you to surrender the rights. These restrictions translate to certain responsibilities for you if you distribute copies of the software, or if you modify it.

For example, if you distribute copies of such a program, whether gratis or for a fee, you must give the recipients all the rights that you have. You must make sure that they, too, receive or can get the source code. And you must show them these terms so they know their rights.

We protect your rights with two steps: (1) copyright the software, and (2) offer you this license which gives you legal permission to copy, distribute and/or modify the software.

Also, for each author's protection and ours, we want to make certain that everyone understands that there is no warranty for this free software. If the software is modified by someone else and passed on, we want its recipients to know that what they have is not the original, so that any problems introduced by others will not reflect on the original authors' reputations.

Finally, any free program is threatened constantly by software patents. We wish to avoid the danger that redistributors of a free program will individually obtain patent licenses, in effect making the program proprietary. To prevent this, we have made it clear that any patent must be licensed for everyone's free use or not licensed at all.

The precise terms and conditions for copying, distribution and modification follow.

TERMS AND CONDITIONS FOR COPYING, DISTRIBUTION AND MODIFICATION

0. This License applies to any program or other work which contains a notice placed by the copyright holder saying it may be distributed under the terms of this General Public License. The "Program", below, refers to any such program or work, and a "work based on the Program" means either the Program or any derivative work under copyright law: that is to say, a work containing the Program or a portion of it, either verbatim or with modifications and/or translated into another language. (Hereinafter, translation is included without limitation in the term "modification".) Each licensee is addressed as "you".

    Activities other than copying, distribution and modification are not covered by this License; they are outside its scope. The act of running the Program is not restricted, and the output from the Program is covered only if its contents constitute a work based on the Program (independent of having been made by running the Program). Whether that is true depends on what the Program does.

1. You may copy and distribute verbatim copies of the Program's source code as you receive it, in any medium, provided that you conspicuously and appropriately publish on each copy an appropriate copyright notice and disclaimer of warranty; keep intact all the notices that refer to this License and to the absence of any warranty; and give any other recipients of the Program a copy of this License along with the Program.

    You may charge a fee for the physical act of transferring a copy, and you may at your option offer warranty protection in exchange for a fee.

2. You may modify your copy or copies of the Program or any portion of it, thus forming a work based on the Program, and copy and distribute such modifications or work under the terms of Section 1 above, provided that you also meet all of these conditions:

    a. You must cause the modified files to carry prominent notices stating that you changed the files and the date of any change.

    b. You must cause any work that you distribute or publish, that in whole or in part contains or is derived from the Program or any part thereof, to be licensed as a whole at no charge to all third parties under the terms of this License.

    c. If the modified program normally reads commands interactively when run, you must cause it, when started running for such interactive use in the most ordinary way, to print or display an announcement including an appropriate copyright notice and a notice that there is no warranty (or else, saying that you provide a warranty) and that users may redistribute the program under these conditions, and telling the user how to view a copy of this License. (Exception: if the Program itself is interactive but does not normally print such an announcement, your work based on the Program is not required to print an announcement.)

These requirements apply to the modified work as a whole. If identifiable sections of that work are not derived from the Program, and can be reasonably considered independent and separate works in themselves, then this License, and its terms, do not apply to those sections when you distribute them as separate works. But when you distribute the same sections as part of a whole which is a work based on the Program, the distribution of the whole must be on the terms of this License, whose permissions for other licensees extend to the entire whole, and thus to each and every part regardless of who wrote it.

Thus, it is not the intent of this section to claim rights or contest your rights to work written entirely by you; rather, the intent is to exercise the right to control the distribution of derivative or collective works based on the Program.

In addition, mere aggregation of another work not based on the Program with the Program (or with a work based on the Program) on a volume of a storage or distribution medium does not bring the other work under the scope of this License.

3. You may copy and distribute the Program (or a work based on it, under Section 2) in object code or executable form under the terms of Sections 1 and 2 above provided that you also do one of the following:

   a. Accompany it with the complete corresponding machine-readable source code, which must be distributed under the terms of Sections 1 and 2 above on a medium customarily used for software interchange; or,

   b. Accompany it with a written offer, valid for at least three years, to give any third party, for a charge no more than your cost of physically performing source distribution, a complete machine-readable copy of the corresponding source code, to be distributed under the terms of Sections 1 and 2 above on a medium customarily used for software interchange; or,

   c. Accompany it with the information you received as to the offer to distribute corresponding source code. (This alternative is allowed only for noncommercial distribution and only if you received the program in object code or executable form with such an offer, in accord with Subsection b above.)

The source code for a work means the preferred form of the work for making modifications to it. For an executable work, complete source code means all the source code for all modules it contains, plus any associated interface definition files, plus the scripts used to control compilation and installation of the executable. However, as a special exception, the source code distributed need not include anything that is normally distributed (in either source or binary form) with the major components (compiler, kernel, and so on) of the operating system on which the executable runs, unless that component itself accompanies the executable.

If distribution of executable or object code is made by offering access to copy from a designated place, then offering equivalent access to copy the source code from the same place counts as distribution of the source code, even though third parties are not compelled to copy the source along with the object code.

4. You may not copy, modify, sublicense, or distribute the Program except as expressly provided under this License. Any attempt otherwise to copy, modify, sublicense or distribute the Program is void, and will automatically terminate your rights under this License. However, parties who have received copies, or rights, from you under this License will not have their licenses terminated so long as such parties remain in full compliance.

5. You are not required to accept this License, since you have not signed it. However, nothing else grants you permission to modify or distribute the Program or its derivative works. These actions are prohibited by law if you do not accept this License. Therefore, by modifying or distributing the Program (or any work based on the Program), you indicate your acceptance of this License to do so, and all its terms and conditions for copying, distributing or modifying the Program or works based on it.

6. Each time you redistribute the Program (or any work based on the Program), the recipient automatically receives a license from the original licensor to copy, distribute or modify the Program subject to these terms and conditions. You may not impose any further restrictions on the recipients' exercise of the rights granted herein. You are not responsible for enforcing compliance by third parties to this License.

7. If, as a consequence of a court judgment or allegation of patent infringement or for any other reason (not limited to patent issues), conditions are imposed on you (whether by court order, agreement or otherwise) that contradict the conditions of this License, they do not excuse you from the conditions of this License. If you cannot distribute so as to satisfy simultaneously your obligations under this License and any other pertinent obligations, then as a consequence you may not distribute the Program at all. For example, if a patent license would not permit royalty-free redistribution of the Program by all those who receive copies directly or indirectly through you, then the only way you could satisfy both it and this License would be to refrain entirely from distribution of the Program.

If any portion of this section is held invalid or unenforceable under any particular circumstance, the balance of the section is intended to apply and the section as a whole is intended to apply in other circumstances.

It is not the purpose of this section to induce you to infringe any patents or other property right claims or to contest validity of any such claims; this section has the sole purpose of protecting the integrity of the free software distribution system, which is implemented by public license practices. Many people have made generous contributions to the wide range of software distributed through that system in reliance on consistent application of that system; it is up to the author/donor to decide if he or she is willing to distribute software through any other system and a licensee cannot impose that choice.

This section is intended to make thoroughly clear what is believed to be a consequence of the rest of this License.

8. If the distribution and/or use of the Program is restricted in certain countries either by patents or by copyrighted interfaces, the original copyright holder who places the Program under this License may add an explicit geographical distribution limitation excluding those countries, so that distribution is permitted only in or among countries not thus excluded. In such case, this License incorporates the limitation as if written in the body of this License.

9. The Free Software Foundation may publish revised and/or new versions of the General Public License from time to time. Such new versions will be similar in spirit to the present version, but may differ in detail to address new problems or concerns.

Each version is given a distinguishing version number. If the Program specifies a version number of this License which applies to it and "any later version", you have the option of following the terms and conditions either of that version or of any later version published by the Free Software Foundation. If the Program does not specify a version number of this License, you may choose any version ever published by the Free Software Foundation.

10. If you wish to incorporate parts of the Program into other free programs whose distribution conditions are different, write to the author to ask for permission. For software which is copyrighted by the Free Software Foundation, write to the Free Software Foundation; we sometimes make exceptions for this. Our decision will be guided by the two goals of preserving the free status of all derivatives of our free software and of promoting the sharing and reuse of software generally.

NO WARRANTY

11. BECAUSE THE PROGRAM IS LICENSED FREE OF CHARGE, THERE IS NO WARRANTY FOR THE PROGRAM, TO THE EXTENT PERMITTED BY APPLICABLE LAW. EXCEPT WHEN OTHERWISE STATED IN WRITING THE COPYRIGHT HOLDERS AND/OR OTHER PARTIES PROVIDE THE PROGRAM "AS IS" WITHOUT WARRANTY OF ANY KIND, EITHER EXPRESSED OR IMPLIED, INCLUDING, BUT NOT LIMITED TO, THE IMPLIED WARRANTIES OF MERCHANTABILITY AND FITNESS FOR A PARTICULAR PURPOSE. THE ENTIRE RISK AS TO THE QUALITY AND PERFORMANCE OF THE PROGRAM IS WITH YOU. SHOULD THE PROGRAM PROVE DEFECTIVE, YOU ASSUME THE COST OF ALL NECESSARY SERVICING, REPAIR OR CORRECTION.

12. IN NO EVENT UNLESS REQUIRED BY APPLICABLE LAW OR AGREED TO IN WRITING WILL ANY COPYRIGHT HOLDER, OR

ANY OTHER PARTY WHO MAY MODIFY AND/OR REDISTRIBUTE
THE PROGRAM AS PERMITTED ABOVE, BE LIABLE TO YOU FOR
DAMAGES, INCLUDING ANY GENERAL, SPECIAL, INCIDENTAL
OR CONSEQUENTIAL DAMAGES ARISING OUT OF THE USE OR
INABILITY TO USE THE PROGRAM (INCLUDING BUT NOT LIMITED
TO LOSS OF DATA OR DATA BEING RENDERED INACCURATE OR
LOSSES SUSTAINED BY YOU OR THIRD PARTIES OR A FAILURE
OF THE PROGRAM TO OPERATE WITH ANY OTHER PROGRAMS),
EVEN IF SUCH HOLDER OR OTHER PARTY HAS BEEN ADVISED OF
THE POSSIBILITY OF SUCH DAMAGES.

END OF TERMS AND CONDITIONS

Appendix: How to Apply These Terms to Your New Programs

If you develop a new program, and you want it to be of the greatest possible use to the public, the best way to achieve this is to make it free software which everyone can redistribute and change under these terms.

To do so, attach the following notices to the program. It is safest to attach them to the start of each source file to most effectively convey the exclusion of warranty; and each file should have at least the "copyright" line and a pointer to where the full notice is found.

```
one line to give the program's name and a brief idea of what it does.
Copyright (C) yyyy   name of author


This program is free software; you can redistribute it and/or modify
it under the terms of the GNU General Public License as published by
the Free Software Foundation; either version 2 of the License, or
(at your option) any later version.


This program is distributed in the hope that it will be useful,
but WITHOUT ANY WARRANTY; without even the implied warranty of
MERCHANTABILITY or FITNESS FOR A PARTICULAR PURPOSE.  See the
GNU General Public License for more details.


You should have received a copy of the GNU General Public License
along with this program; if not, write to the Free Software
Foundation, Inc., 59 Temple Place - Suite 330, Boston, MA  02111-1307, USA.
```

Also add information on how to contact you by electronic and paper mail.

If the program is interactive, make it output a short notice like this when it starts in an interactive mode:

```
Gnomovision version 69, Copyright (C) 19yy  name of author
Gnomovision comes with ABSOLUTELY NO WARRANTY; for details type 'show w'.
This is free software, and you are welcome to redistribute it
under certain conditions; type 'show c' for details.
```

The hypothetical commands 'show w' and 'show c' should show the appropriate parts of the General Public License. Of course, the commands you use may be called something other than 'show w' and 'show c'; they could even be mouse-clicks or menu items—whatever suits your program.

You should also get your employer (if you work as a programmer) or your school, if any, to sign a "copyright disclaimer" for the program, if necessary. Here is a sample; alter the names:

```
Yoyodyne, Inc., hereby disclaims all copyright interest in the program
'Gnomovision' (which makes passes at compilers) written by James Hacker.
```

signature of Ty Coon, 1 April 1989

`Ty Coon, President of Vice`

This General Public License does not permit incorporating your program into proprietary programs. If your program is a subroutine library, you may consider it more useful to permit linking proprietary applications with the library. If this is what you want to do, use the GNU Library General Public License instead of this License.

1 The Concepts of Bison

This chapter introduces many of the basic concepts without which the details of Bison will not make sense. If you do not already know how to use Bison or Yacc, we suggest you start by reading this chapter carefully.

1.1 Languages and Context-Free Grammars

In order for Bison to parse a language, it must be described by a *context-free grammar*. This means that you specify one or more *syntactic groupings* and give rules for constructing them from their parts. For example, in the C language, one kind of grouping is called an 'expression'. One rule for making an expression might be, "An expression can be made of a minus sign and another expression". Another would be, "An expression can be an integer". As you can see, rules are often recursive, but there must be at least one rule which leads out of the recursion.

The most common formal system for presenting such rules for humans to read is *Backus-Naur Form* or "BNF", which was developed in order to specify the language Algol 60. Any grammar expressed in BNF is a context-free grammar. The input to Bison is essentially machine-readable BNF.

There are various important subclasses of context-free grammar. Although it can handle almost all context-free grammars, Bison is optimized for what are called LALR(1) grammars. In brief, in these grammars, it must be possible to tell how to parse any portion of an input string with just a single token of look-ahead. Strictly speaking, that is a description of an LR(1) grammar, and LALR(1) involves additional restrictions that are hard to explain simply; but it is rare in actual practice to find an LR(1) grammar that fails to be LALR(1). See Section 5.7 [Mysterious Reduce/Reduce Conflicts], page 80, for more information on this.

Parsers for LALR(1) grammars are *deterministic*, meaning roughly that the next grammar rule to apply at any point in the input is uniquely determined by the preceding input and a fixed, finite portion (called a *look-ahead*) of the remaining input. A context-free grammar can be *ambiguous*, meaning that there are multiple ways to apply the grammar rules to get the same inputs. Even unambiguous grammars can be *nondeterministic*, meaning that no fixed look-ahead always suffices to determine the next grammar rule to apply. With the proper declarations, Bison is also able to parse these more general context-free grammars, using a technique known as GLR parsing (for Generalized LR). Bison's GLR parsers are able to handle any context-free grammar for which the number of possible parses of any given string is finite.

In the formal grammatical rules for a language, each kind of syntactic unit or grouping is named by a *symbol*. Those which are built by grouping smaller constructs according to grammatical rules are called *nonterminal symbols*; those which can't be subdivided are called *terminal symbols* or *token types*. We call a piece of input corresponding to a single terminal symbol a *token*, and a piece corresponding to a single nonterminal symbol a *grouping*.

We can use the C language as an example of what symbols, terminal and non-terminal, mean. The tokens of C are identifiers, constants (numeric and string), and the various keywords, arithmetic operators and punctuation marks. So the terminal symbols of a grammar for C include 'identifier', 'number' and 'string', plus one symbol for each keyword, operator or punctuation mark: 'if', 'return', 'const', 'static', 'int', 'char', 'plus-sign', 'open-brace', 'close-brace', 'comma' and many more. (These tokens can be subdivided into characters, but that is a matter of lexicography, not grammar.)

Here is a simple C function subdivided into tokens:

```
int                /* keyword 'int' */
square (int x)     /* identifier, open-paren, identifier, identifier, close-paren */
{                  /* open-brace */
   return x * x;   /* keyword 'return', identifier, asterisk, identifier, semicolon */
}                  /* close-brace */
```

The syntactic groupings of C include the expression, the statement, the declaration, and the function definition. These are represented in the grammar of C by the nonterminal symbols 'expression', 'statement', 'declaration' and 'function definition'. The full grammar uses dozens of additional language constructs, each with its own nonterminal symbol, in order to express the meanings of these four. The example above is a function definition; it contains one declaration and one statement. In the statement, each 'x' is an expression, as is 'x * x'.

Each nonterminal symbol must have grammatical rules showing how it is made out of simpler constructs. For example, one kind of C statement is the `return` statement; this would be described with a grammar rule which reads informally as:

A 'statement' can be made of a 'return' keyword, an 'expression' and a 'semicolon'.

There would be many other rules for 'statement'; one for each kind of statement in C.

One nonterminal symbol must be distinguished as the special one which defines a complete utterance in the language. It is called the *start symbol*. In a compiler, this means a complete input program. In the C language, the nonterminal symbol 'sequence of definitions and declarations' plays this role.

For example, '1 + 2' is a valid C expression—a valid part of a C program—but it is not valid as an *entire* C program. In the context-free grammar of C, this follows from the fact that 'expression' is not the start-symbol.

The Bison parser reads a sequence of tokens as its input, and groups the tokens using the grammar rules. If the input is valid, the end result is that the entire token sequence reduces to a single grouping whose symbol is the grammar's start-symbol. If we use a grammar for C, the entire input must be a 'sequence of definitions and declarations'. If not, the parser reports a syntax error.

1.2 From Formal Rules to Bison Input

A formal grammar is a mathematical construct. To define the language for Bison, you must write a file expressing the grammar in Bison syntax: a *Bison grammar* file (see Chapter 3 [Bison Grammar Files], page 43).

A nonterminal symbol in the formal grammar is represented in Bison input as an identifier, like an identifier in C. By convention, it should be in lowercase, such as expr, stmt or declaration.

The Bison representation for a terminal symbol is also called a *token type*. Token types can be represented as C-like identifiers as well. By convention, these identifiers should be in uppercase to distinguish them from nonterminals: for example, INTEGER, IDENTIFIER, IF or RETURN. A terminal symbol that stands for a particular keyword in the language should be named after that keyword converted to uppercase. The terminal symbol error is reserved for error recovery (see Section 3.2 [Symbols], page 44).

A terminal symbol can also be represented as a character literal, just like a C character constant. You should do this whenever a token is just a single character (parenthesis, plus-sign, etc.): use that same character in a literal as the terminal symbol for that token.

A third way to represent a terminal symbol is with a C string constant containing several characters (see Section 3.2 [Symbols], page 44).

The grammar rules also have an expression in Bison syntax. For example, here is the Bison rule for a C return statement (the semicolon in quotes is a literal character token, representing part of the C syntax for the statement; the naked semicolon, and the colon, are Bison punctuation used in every rule):

```
stmt:    RETURN expr ';'
         ;
```

For more information, see Section 3.3 [Syntax of Grammar Rules], page 47.

1.3 Semantic Values

A formal grammar selects tokens only by their classifications. For example, if a rule mentions the terminal symbol 'integer constant', it means that *any* integer constant is grammatically valid in that position. The precise value of the constant is irrelevant to how to parse the input: if 'x+4' is grammatical then 'x+1' or 'x+3989' is equally grammatical.

But the precise value is very important for what the input means once it is parsed. A compiler is useless if it fails to distinguish between 4, 1 and 3989 as constants in the program! Therefore, each token in a Bison grammar has both a token type and a *semantic value* (see Section 3.5 [Defining Language Semantics], page 48.

The token type is a terminal symbol defined in the grammar, such as INTEGER, IDENTIFIER or ','. It tells everything you need to know to decide where the token may validly appear and how to group it with other tokens. The grammar rules know nothing about tokens except their types.

The semantic value has all the rest of the information about the meaning of the token, such as the value of an integer, or the name of an identifier. (A token such as ',' that is just punctuation doesn't need to have any semantic value.)

For example, an input token might be classified as token type INTEGER and have the semantic value 4. Another input token might have the same token type INTEGER but value 3989. When a grammar rule says that INTEGER is allowed, either of these tokens is acceptable because each is an INTEGER. When the parser accepts the token, it keeps track of the token's semantic value.

Each grouping can also have a semantic value as well as its nonterminal symbol. For example, in a calculator, an expression typically has a semantic value that is a number. In a compiler for a programming language, an expression typically has a semantic value that is a tree structure describing the meaning of the expression.

1.4 Semantic Actions

In order to be useful, a program must do more than parse input; it must also produce some output based on the input. In a Bison grammar, a grammar rule can have an *action* made up of C statements. Each time the parser recognizes a match for that rule, the action is executed (see Section 3.5.3 [Actions], page 49).

Most of the time, the purpose of an action is to compute the semantic value of the whole construct from the semantic values of its parts. For example, suppose we have a rule which says an expression can be the sum of two expressions. When the parser recognizes such a sum, each of the subexpressions has a semantic value which describes how it was built up. The action for this rule should create a similar sort of value for the newly recognized larger expression.

For example, here is a rule that says an expression can be the sum of two subexpressions:

```
expr: expr '+' expr    { $$ = $1 + $3; }
    ;
```

The action says how to produce the semantic value of the sum expression from the values of the two subexpressions.

1.5 Writing GLR Parsers

In some grammars, there will be cases where Bison's standard LALR(1) parsing algorithm cannot decide whether to apply a certain grammar rule at a given point. That is, it may not be able to decide (on the basis of the input read so far) which of two possible reductions (applications of a grammar rule) applies, or whether to apply a reduction or read more of the input and apply a reduction later in the input. These are known respectively as *reduce/reduce* conflicts (see Section 5.6 [Reduce/Reduce], page 78), and *shift/reduce* conflicts (see Section 5.2 [Shift/Reduce], page 74).

To use a grammar that is not easily modified to be LALR(1), a more general parsing algorithm is sometimes necessary. If you include `%glr-parser` among the Bison declarations in your file (see Section 3.1 [Grammar Outline], page 43), the result will be a Generalized LR (GLR) parser. These parsers handle Bison grammars that contain no unresolved conflicts (i.e., after applying precedence declarations) identically to LALR(1) parsers. However, when faced with unresolved shift/reduce and reduce/reduce conflicts, GLR parsers use the simple expedient of doing both, effectively cloning the parser to follow both possibilities. Each of the resulting parsers can again split, so that at any given time, there can be any number of possible parses being explored. The parsers proceed in lock-step; that is, all of them consume (shift) a given input symbol before any of them proceed to the next. Each of the cloned parsers eventually meets one of two possible fates: either it runs into a parsing error, in which case it simply vanishes, or it merges with another parser, because the two of them have reduced the input to an identical set of symbols.

During the time that there are multiple parsers, semantic actions are recorded, but not performed. When a parser disappears, its recorded semantic actions disappear as well, and are never performed. When a reduction makes two parsers identical, causing them to merge, Bison records both sets of semantic actions. Whenever the last two parsers merge, reverting to the single-parser case, Bison resolves all the outstanding actions either by precedences given to the grammar rules involved, or by performing both actions, and then calling a designated user-defined function on the resulting values to produce an arbitrary merged result.

Let's consider an example, vastly simplified from a C++ grammar.

```
%{
  #include <stdio.h>
  #define YYSTYPE char const *
  int yylex (void);
  void yyerror (char const *);
%}

%token TYPENAME ID

%right '='
%left '+'

%glr-parser

%%

prog :
     | prog stmt    { printf ("\n"); }
     ;

stmt : expr ';'   %dprec 1
```

```
            | decl      %dprec 2
            ;


    expr : ID                    { printf ("%s ", $$); }
         | TYPENAME '(' expr ')'
                                 { printf ("%s <cast> ", $1); }
         | expr '+' expr  { printf ("+ "); }
         | expr '=' expr  { printf ("= "); }
         ;


    decl : TYPENAME declarator ';'
                                 { printf ("%s <declare> ", $1); }
         | TYPENAME declarator '=' expr ';'
                                 { printf ("%s <init-declare> ", $1); }
         ;


    declarator : ID        { printf ("\"%s\" ", $1); }
               | '(' declarator ')'
               ;
```

This models a problematic part of the C++ grammar—the ambiguity between certain declarations and statements. For example:

```
    T (x) = y+z;
```

parses as either an `expr` or a `stmt` (assuming that 'T' is recognized as a TYPENAME and 'x' as an ID). Bison detects this as a reduce/reduce conflict between the rules `expr : ID` and `declarator : ID`, which it cannot resolve at the time it encounters x in the example above. The two `%dprec` declarations, however, give precedence to interpreting the example as a `decl`, which implies that x is a declarator. The parser therefore prints:

```
    "x" y z + T <init-declare>
```

Consider a different input string for this parser:

```
    T (x) + y;
```

Here, there is no ambiguity (this cannot be parsed as a declaration). However, at the time the Bison parser encounters x, it does not have enough information to resolve the reduce/reduce conflict (again, between x as an `expr` or a `declarator`). In this case, no precedence declaration is used. Instead, the parser splits into two, one assuming that x is an `expr`, and the other that x is a `declarator`. The second of these parsers then vanishes when it sees +, and the parser prints:

```
    x T <cast> y +
```

Suppose that instead of resolving the ambiguity, you wanted to see all the possibilities. For this purpose, we must *merge* the semantic actions of the two possible parsers, rather than choosing one over the other. To do so, you could change the declaration of `stmt` as follows:

```
    stmt : expr ';'  %merge <stmtMerge>
```

```
     | decl        %merge <stmtMerge>
     ;
```

and define the `stmtMerge` function as:

```
static YYSTYPE
stmtMerge (YYSTYPE x0, YYSTYPE x1)
{
  printf ("<OR> ");
  return "";
}
```

with an accompanying forward declaration in the C declarations at the beginning of the file:

```
%{
  #define YYSTYPE char const *
  static YYSTYPE stmtMerge (YYSTYPE x0, YYSTYPE x1);
%}
```

With these declarations, the resulting parser will parse the first example as both an `expr` and a `decl`, and print:

```
"x" y z + T <init-declare> x T <cast> y z + = <OR>
```

The GLR parsers require a compiler for ISO C89 or later. In addition, they use the `inline` keyword, which is not C89, but is C99 and is a common extension in pre-C99 compilers. It is up to the user of these parsers to handle portability issues. For instance, if using Autoconf and the Autoconf macro `AC_C_INLINE`, a mere:

```
%{
  #include <config.h>
%}
```

will suffice. Otherwise, we suggest:

```
%{
  #if __STDC_VERSION__ < 199901 && ! defined __GNUC__ && ! defined inline
   #define inline
  #endif
%}
```

1.6 Locations

Many applications, like interpreters or compilers, have to produce verbose and useful error messages. To achieve this, one must be able to keep track of the *textual location*, or *location*, of each syntactic construct. Bison provides a mechanism for handling these locations.

Each token has a semantic value. In a similar fashion, each token has an associated location, but the type of location is the same for all tokens and groupings.

Moreover, the output parser is equipped with a default data structure for storing locations (see Section 3.6 [Locations], page 53).

Like semantic values, locations can be reached in actions using a dedicated set of constructs. In the example above, the location of the whole grouping is @$, while the locations of the subexpressions are @1 and @3.

When a rule is matched, a default action is used to compute the semantic value of its left hand side (see Section 3.5.3 [Actions], page 49). In the same way, another default action is used for locations. However, the action for locations is general enough for most cases, meaning there is usually no need to describe for each rule how @$ should be formed. When building a new location for a given grouping, the default behavior of the output parser is to take the beginning of the first symbol, and the end of the last symbol.

1.7 Bison Output: the Parser File

When you run Bison, you give it a Bison grammar file as input. The output is a C source file that parses the language described by the grammar. This file is called a *Bison parser*. Keep in mind that the Bison utility and the Bison parser are two distinct programs: the Bison utility is a program whose output is the Bison parser that becomes part of your program.

The job of the Bison parser is to group tokens into groupings according to the grammar rules—for example, to build identifiers and operators into expressions. As it does this, it runs the actions for the grammar rules it uses.

The tokens come from a function called the *lexical analyzer* that you must supply in some fashion (such as by writing it in C). The Bison parser calls the lexical analyzer each time it wants a new token. It doesn't know what is "inside" the tokens (though their semantic values may reflect this). Typically the lexical analyzer makes the tokens by parsing characters of text, but Bison does not depend on this (see Section 4.2 [The Lexical Analyzer Function yylex], page 66.

The Bison parser file is C code which defines a function named yyparse which implements that grammar. This function does not make a complete C program; you must supply some additional functions. One is the lexical analyzer. Another is an error-reporting function which the parser calls to report an error. In addition, a complete C program must start with a function called main; you have to provide this, and arrange for it to call yyparse or the parser will never run (see Chapter 4 [Parser C-Language Interface], page 65.

Aside from the token type names and the symbols in the actions you write, all symbols defined in the Bison parser file itself begin with 'yy' or 'YY'. This includes interface functions such as the lexical analyzer function yylex, the error-reporting function yyerror and the parser function yyparse itself. This also includes numerous identifiers used for internal purposes. Therefore, you should avoid using C identifiers starting with 'yy' or 'YY' in the Bison grammar file except for the ones defined in this manual.

In some cases the Bison parser file includes system headers, and in those cases your code should respect the identifiers reserved by those headers. On some non-GNU hosts, `<alloca.h>`, `<stddef.h>`, and `<stdlib.h>` are included as needed to declare memory allocators and related types. Other system headers may be included if you define `YYDEBUG` to a nonzero value (see Section 8.2 [Tracing Your Parser], page 97).

1.8 Stages in Using Bison

The actual language design process using Bison, from grammar specification to a working compiler or interpreter, has these parts:

1. Formally specify the grammar in a form recognized by Bison (see Chapter 3 [Bison Grammar Files], page 43). For each grammatical rule in the language, describe the action that is to be taken when an instance of that rule is recognized. The action is described by a sequence of C statements.

2. Write a lexical analyzer to process input and pass tokens to the parser. The lexical analyzer may be written by hand in C (see Section 4.2 [The Lexical Analyzer Function `yylex`], page 66). It could also be produced using Lex, but the use of Lex is not discussed in this manual.

3. Write a controlling function that calls the Bison-produced parser.

4. Write error-reporting routines.

To turn this source code as written into a usable program, you must follow these steps:

1. Run Bison on the grammar to produce the parser.

2. Compile the code output by Bison, as well as any other source files.

3. Link the object files to produce the finished product.

1.9 The Overall Layout of a Bison Grammar

The input file for the Bison utility is a *Bison grammar file*. The general form of a Bison grammar file is as follows:

```
%{
Prologue
%}

Bison declarations

%%
Grammar rules
%%
Epilogue
```

The '`%%`', '`%{`' and '`%}`' are punctuation marks which appear in every Bison grammar file to separate the sections.

The prologue may define types and variables used in the actions. You can also use preprocessor commands to define macros used there, and use `#include` to include header files that do any of these things. You need to declare the lexical analyzer `yylex` and the error printer `yyerror` here, along with any other global identifiers used by the actions in the grammar rules.

The Bison declarations declare the names of the terminal and nonterminal symbols, and may also describe operator precedence and the data types of semantic values of various symbols.

The grammar rules define how to construct each nonterminal symbol from its parts.

The epilogue can contain any code you want to use. Often the definitions of functions declared in the prologue go here. In a simple program, all the rest of the program can go here.

2 Examples

Now we show and explain three sample programs written using Bison: a reverse polish notation calculator, an algebraic (infix) notation calculator, and a multifunction calculator. All three have been tested under BSD Unix 4.3; each produces a usable, though limited, interactive desktop calculator.

These examples are simple, but Bison grammars for real programming languages are written the same way.

2.1 Reverse Polish Notation Calculator

The first example is that of a simple double-precision *reverse polish notation* calculator (a calculator using postfix operators). This example provides a good starting point, since operator precedence is not an issue. The second example will illustrate how operator precedence is handled.

The source code for this calculator is named 'rpcalc.y'. The '.y' extension is a convention used for Bison input files.

2.1.1 Declarations for `rpcalc`

Here are the C and Bison declarations for the reverse polish notation calculator. As in C, comments are placed between '/* ... */'.

```
/* Reverse polish notation calculator.  */

%{
  #define YYSTYPE double
  #include <math.h>
  int yylex (void);
  void yyerror (char const *);
%}

%token NUM

%% /* Grammar rules and actions follow.  */
```

The declarations section (see Section 3.1.1 [The prologue], page 43) contains two preprocessor directives and two forward declarations.

The #define directive defines the macro YYSTYPE, thus specifying the C data type for semantic values of both tokens and groupings (see Section 3.5.1 [Data Types of Semantic Values], page 49). The Bison parser will use whatever type YYSTYPE is defined as; if you don't define it, int is the default. Because we specify double, each token and each expression has an associated value, which is a floating point number.

The #include directive is used to declare the exponentiation function pow.

The forward declarations for `yylex` and `yyerror` are needed because the C language requires that functions be declared before they are used. These functions will be defined in the epilogue, but since the parser calls them, they must be declared in the prologue.

The second section, Bison declarations, provides information to Bison about the token types. (See Section 3.1.2 [The Bison Declarations Section], page 44.) Each terminal symbol that is not a single-character literal must be declared here. (Single-character literals normally don't need to be declared.) In this example, all the arithmetic operators are designated by single-character literals, so the only terminal symbol that needs to be declared is NUM, the token type for numeric constants.

2.1.2 Grammar Rules for `rpcalc`

Here are the grammar rules for the reverse polish notation calculator:

```
input:    /* empty */
        | input line

;


line:     '\n'
        | exp '\n'        { printf ("\t%.10g\n", $1); }

;


exp:      NUM             { $$ = $1;                }
        | exp exp '+'     { $$ = $1 + $2;           }
        | exp exp '-'     { $$ = $1 - $2;           }
        | exp exp '*'     { $$ = $1 * $2;           }
        | exp exp '/'     { $$ = $1 / $2;           }
        /* Exponentiation */
        | exp exp '^'     { $$ = pow ($1, $2); }
        /* Unary minus    */
        | exp 'n'         { $$ = -$1;               }

;
%%
```

The groupings of the rpcalc "language" defined here are the expression (given the name `exp`), the line of input (`line`), and the complete input transcript (`input`). Each of these nonterminal symbols has several alternate rules, joined by the '|' punctuation mark, which is read as "or". The following sections explain what these rules mean.

The semantics of the language is determined by the actions taken when a grouping is recognized. The actions are the C code that appears inside braces. (See Section 3.5.3 [Actions], page 49.)

You must specify these actions in C, but Bison provides the means for passing semantic values between the rules. In each action, the pseudo-variable $$ stands for the semantic value for the grouping that the rule is going to construct. Assigning a value to $$ is the main job of most actions. The semantic values of the components of the rule are referred to as $1, $2, and so on.

2.1.2.1 Explanation of `input`

Consider the definition of `input`:

```
input:    /* empty */
        | input line

    ;
```

This definition reads as follows: "A complete input is either an empty string, or a complete input followed by an input line". Notice that "complete input" is defined in terms of itself. This definition is said to be *left recursive* since `input` appears always as the symbol farthest to the left in the sequence. (See Section 3.4 [Recursive Rules], page 48.)

The first alternative is empty because there are no symbols between the colon and the first '|'; this means that `input` can match an empty string of input (no tokens). We write the rules this way because it is legitimate to type *Ctrl-d* right after you start the calculator. The convention is to put an empty alternative first and write the comment '/* empty */' in it.

The second alternate rule (`input line`) handles all nontrivial input. It means, "After reading any number of lines, read one more line if possible". The left recursion makes this rule into a loop. Since the first alternative matches empty input, the loop can be executed zero or more times.

The parser function `yyparse` continues to process input until a grammatical error is seen or the lexical analyzer says there are no more input tokens; we will arrange for the latter to happen at end-of-input.

2.1.2.2 Explanation of `line`

Now consider the definition of `line`:

```
line:     '\n'
        | exp '\n'  { printf ("\t%.10g\n", $1); }

    ;
```

The first alternative is a token which is a newline character; this means that rpcalc accepts a blank line (and ignores it, since there is no action). The second alternative is an expression followed by a newline. This is the alternative that makes rpcalc useful. The semantic value of the `exp` grouping is the value of $1 because the `exp` in question is the first symbol in the alternative. The action prints this value, which is the result of the computation the user asked for.

This action is unusual because it does not assign a value to $$. As a consequence, the semantic value associated with the `line` is uninitialized (its value will be unpredictable). This would be a bug if that value were ever used, but we don't use it: once rpcalc has printed the value of the user's input line, that value is no longer needed.

2.1.2.3 Explanation of `expr`

The `exp` grouping has several rules, one for each kind of expression. The first rule handles the simplest expressions: those that are just numbers. The second handles an addition-expression, which looks like two expressions followed by a plus-sign. The third handles subtraction, and so on.

```
exp:      NUM
    | exp exp '+'      { $$ = $1 + $2;      }
    | exp exp '-'      { $$ = $1 - $2;      }
    ...
    ;
```

We have used '|' to join all the rules for `exp`, but we could equally well have written them separately:

```
exp:      NUM ;
exp:      exp exp '+'      { $$ = $1 + $2;      } ;
exp:      exp exp '-'      { $$ = $1 - $2;      } ;
    ...
```

Most of the rules have actions that compute the value of the expression in terms of the value of its parts. For example, in the rule for addition, $1 refers to the first component `exp` and $2 refers to the second one. The third component, '+', has no meaningful associated semantic value, but if it had one you could refer to it as $3. When `yyparse` recognizes a sum expression using this rule, the sum of the two subexpressions' values is produced as the value of the entire expression. (See Section 3.5.3 [Actions], page 49.)

You don't have to give an action for every rule. When a rule has no action, Bison by default copies the value of $1 into $$. This is what happens in the first rule (the one that uses NUM).

The formatting shown here is the recommended convention, but Bison does not require it. You can add or change white space as much as you wish. For example, this:

```
exp   : NUM | exp exp '+' {$$ = $1 + $2; } | ...
```
means the same thing as this:

```
exp:      NUM
    | exp exp '+'      { $$ = $1 + $2; }
    | ...
```
The latter, however, is much more readable.

2.1.3 The `rpcalc` Lexical Analyzer

The lexical analyzer's job is low-level parsing: converting characters or sequences of characters into tokens. The Bison parser gets its tokens by calling the lexical analyzer. (See Section 4.2 [The Lexical Analyzer Function `yylex`], page 66.)

Only a simple lexical analyzer is needed for the RPN calculator. This lexical analyzer skips blanks and tabs, then reads in numbers as `double` and returns them as NUM tokens. Any other character that isn't part of a number is a separate token. Note that the token code for such a single-character token is the character itself.

The return value of the lexical analyzer function is a numeric code which represents a token type. The same text used in Bison rules to stand for this token type is also a C expression for the numeric code for this type. This works in two ways. If the token type is a character literal, then its numeric code is that of the character; you can use the same character literal in the lexical analyzer to express the number. If the token type is an identifier, that identifier is defined by Bison as a C macro whose definition is the appropriate number. In this example, therefore, NUM becomes a macro for `yylex` to use.

The semantic value of the token (if it has one) is stored into the global variable `yylval`, which is where the Bison parser will look for it. (The C data type of `yylval` is YYSTYPE, which was defined at the beginning of the grammar; see Section 2.1.1 [Declarations for `rpcalc`], page 23.)

A token type code of zero is returned if the end-of-input is encountered. (Bison recognizes any nonpositive value as indicating end-of-input.)

Here is the code for the lexical analyzer:

```
/* The lexical analyzer returns a double floating point
   number on the stack and the token NUM, or the numeric code
   of the character read if not a number.  It skips all blanks
   and tabs, and returns 0 for end-of-input.  */

#include <ctype.h>
int
yylex (void)
{
  int c;

  /* Skip white space.  */
  while ((c = getchar ()) == ' ' || c == '\t')
    ;
  /* Process numbers.  */
  if (c == '.' || isdigit (c))
    {
      ungetc (c, stdin);
      scanf ("%lf", &yylval);
      return NUM;
    }
```

```
/* Return end-of-input.  */
if (c == EOF)
  return 0;
/* Return a single char.  */
return c;
}
```

2.1.4 The Controlling Function

In keeping with the spirit of this example, the controlling function is kept to the bare minimum. The only requirement is that it call yyparse to start the process of parsing.

```
int
main (void)
{
  return yyparse ();
}
```

2.1.5 The Error Reporting Routine

When yyparse detects a syntax error, it calls the error reporting function yyerror to print an error message (usually but not always "syntax error"). It is up to the programmer to supply yyerror (see Chapter 4 [Parser C-Language Interface], page 65), so here is the definition we will use:

```
#include <stdio.h>

/* Called by yyparse on error.  */
void
yyerror (char const *s)
{
  printf ("%s\n", s);
}
```

After yyerror returns, the Bison parser may recover from the error and continue parsing if the grammar contains a suitable error rule. (See Chapter 6 [Error Recovery], page 85.) Otherwise, yyparse returns nonzero. We have not written any error rules in this example, so any invalid input will cause the calculator program to exit. This is not clean behavior for a real calculator, but it is adequate for the first example.

2.1.6 Running Bison to Make the Parser

Before running Bison to produce a parser, we need to decide how to arrange all the source code in one or more source files. For such a simple example, the easiest thing is to put everything in one file. The definitions of yylex, yyerror and main go at the end, in the epilogue of the file (see Section 1.9 [The Overall Layout of a Bison Grammar], page 21).

For a large project, you would probably have several source files, and use make to arrange to recompile them.

With all the source in a single file, you use the following command to convert it into a parser file:

```
bison file_name.y
```

In this example the file was called 'rpcalc.y' (for "Reverse Polish CALCulator"). Bison produces a file named 'file_name.tab.c', removing the '.y' from the original file name. The file output by Bison contains the source code for yyparse. The additional functions in the input file (yylex, yyerror and main) are copied verbatim to the output.

2.1.7 Compiling the Parser File

Here is how to compile and run the parser file:

List the files in the current directory.

```
$ ls
rpcalc.tab.c   rpcalc.y
```

Compile the Bison parser. '-lm' tells the compiler to search the math library for pow.

```
$ cc -lm -o rpcalc rpcalc.tab.c
```

List the files again.

```
$ ls
rpcalc   rpcalc.tab.c   rpcalc.y
```

The file 'rpcalc' now contains the executable code. Here is an example session using rpcalc.

```
$ rpcalc
4 9 +
13
3 7 + 3 4 5 *+-
-13
3 7 + 3 4 5 * + - n          Note the unary minus, 'n'
13
5 6 / 4 n +
-3.166666667
3 4 ^                        Exponentiation
81
^D                           End-of-file indicator
$
```

2.2 Infix Notation Calculator: `calc`

We now modify `rpcalc` to handle infix operators instead of postfix. Infix notation involves the concept of operator precedence and the need for parentheses nested to an arbitrary depth. Here is the Bison code for 'calc.y', an infix desktop calculator:

```
/* Infix notation calculator.  */

%{
  #define YYSTYPE double
  #include <math.h>
  #include <stdio.h>
  int yylex (void);
  void yyerror (char const *);
%}

/* Bison declarations.  */
%token NUM
%left '-' '+'
%left '*' '/'
%left NEG     /* negation--unary minus */
%right '^'    /* exponentiation */

%% /* The grammar follows.  */
input:   /* empty */
       | input line
;

line:    '\n'
       | exp '\n'  { printf ("\t%.10g\n", $1); }
;

exp:     NUM                  { $$ = $1;          }
       | exp '+' exp          { $$ = $1 + $3;     }
       | exp '-' exp          { $$ = $1 - $3;     }
       | exp '*' exp          { $$ = $1 * $3;     }
       | exp '/' exp          { $$ = $1 / $3;     }
       | '-' exp %prec NEG { $$ = -$2;            }
       | exp '^' exp          { $$ = pow ($1, $3); }
       | '(' exp ')'          { $$ = $2;          }
;
%%
```

The functions `yylex`, `yyerror` and `main` can be the same as before.

There are two important new features shown in this code.

In the second section (Bison declarations), `%left` declares token types and says they are left-associative operators. The declarations `%left` and `%right` (right associativity) take the place of `%token`, which is used to declare a token type name without associativity. (These tokens are single-character literals, which ordinarily don't need to be declared. We declare them here to specify the associativity.)

Operator precedence is determined by the line ordering of the declarations; the higher the line number of the declaration (lower on the page or screen), the higher the precedence. Hence, exponentiation has the highest precedence, unary minus (NEG) is next, followed by '`*`' and '`/`', and so on. (See Section 5.3 [Operator Precedence], page 75.)

The other important new feature is the `%prec` in the grammar section for the unary minus operator. The `%prec` simply instructs Bison that the rule '`| '-'` exp' has the same precedence as NEG—in this case the next-to-highest. (See Section 5.4 [Context-Dependent Precedence], page 77.)

Here is a sample run of '`calc.y`':

```
$ calc
4 + 4.5 - (34/(8*3+-3))
6.880952381
-56 + 2
-54
3 ^ 2
9
```

2.3 Simple Error Recovery

Up to this point, this manual has not addressed the issue of *error recovery*—how to continue parsing after the parser detects a syntax error. All we have handled is error reporting with `yyerror`. Recall that by default `yyparse` returns after calling `yyerror`. This means that an erroneous input line causes the calculator program to exit. Now we show how to rectify this deficiency.

The Bison language itself includes the reserved word `error`, which may be included in the grammar rules. In the example below, it has been added to one of the alternatives for `line`:

```
line:     '\n'
        | exp '\n'   { printf ("\t%.10g\n", $1); }
        | error '\n' { yyerrok;                  }
    ;
```

This addition to the grammar allows for simple error recovery in the event of a syntax error. If an expression that cannot be evaluated is read, the error will be recognized by the third rule for `line`, and parsing will continue. (The `yyerror` function is still called upon to print its message as well.) The action executes the statement `yyerrok`, a macro defined automatically by Bison; its meaning is that error recovery is complete (see Chapter 6 [Error Recovery], page 85). Note the difference between `yyerrok` and `yyerror`; neither one is a misprint.

This form of error recovery deals with syntax errors. There are other kinds of errors; for example, division by zero, which raises an exception signal that is normally fatal. A real calculator program must handle this signal and use `longjmp` to return to `main` and resume parsing input lines; it would also have to discard the rest of the current line of input. We won't discuss this issue further because it is not specific to Bison programs.

2.4 Location Tracking Calculator: `ltcalc`

This example extends the infix notation calculator with location tracking. This feature will be used to improve the error messages. For the sake of clarity, this example is a simple integer calculator, since most of the work needed to use locations will be done in the lexical analyzer.

2.4.1 Declarations for `ltcalc`

The C and Bison declarations for the location tracking calculator are the same as the declarations for the infix notation calculator.

```
/* Location tracking calculator.  */

%{
  #define YYSTYPE int
  #include <math.h>
  int yylex (void);
  void yyerror (char const *);
%}

/* Bison declarations.  */
%token NUM

%left '-' '+'
%left '*' '/'
%left NEG
%right '^'

%% /* The grammar follows.  */
```

Note there are no declarations specific to locations. Defining a data type for storing locations is not needed: we will use the type provided by default (see Section 3.6.1 [Data Types of Locations], page 53), which is a four member structure with the following integer fields: `first_line`, `first_column`, `last_line` and `last_column`.

2.4.2 Grammar Rules for `ltcalc`

Whether the calculator is handling locations or not has no effect on the syntax of your language. Therefore, grammar rules for this example will be very close to those of the previous example; we will only modify them to benefit from the new information.

Here, we will use locations to report divisions by zero, and locate the wrong expressions or subexpressions.

```
input    : /* empty */
         | input line
         ;

line     : '\n'
         | exp '\n'  { printf ("%d\n", $1); }
         ;

exp      : NUM              { $$ = $1; }
         | exp '+' exp      { $$ = $1 + $3; }
         | exp '-' exp      { $$ = $1 - $3; }
         | exp '*' exp      { $$ = $1 * $3; }
         | exp '/' exp
            {
              if ($3)
                $$ = $1 / $3;
              else
                {
                  $$ = 1;
                  fprintf (stderr, "%d.%d-%d.%d: division by zero",
                           @3.first_line, @3.first_column,
                           @3.last_line, @3.last_column);
                }
            }
         | '-' exp %preg NEG    { $$ = -$2; }
         | exp '^' exp          { $$ = pow ($1, $3); }
         | '(' exp ')'          { $$ = $2; }
```

This code shows how to reach locations inside of semantic actions, by using the pseudo-variables @*n* for rule components, and the pseudo-variable @$ for groupings.

We don't need to assign a value to @$: the output parser does it automatically. By default, before executing the C code of each action, @$ is set to range from the beginning of @1 to the end of @*n*, for a rule with *n* components. This behavior can be redefined (see Section 3.6.3 [Default Action for Locations], page 55), and for very specific rules, @$ can be computed by hand.

2.4.3 The `ltcalc` Lexical Analyzer.

Until now we relied on Bison's defaults to enable location tracking. The next step is to rewrite the lexical analyzer, enabling it to feed the locations of tokens to the parser as it already does with semantic values. To ensure the precision of the computed locations, we must take into account every character of the input text.

```
int
yylex (void)
{
  int c;

  /* Skip white space.  */
  while ((c = getchar ()) == ' ' || c == '\t')
    ++yylloc.last_column;

  /* Step.  */
  yylloc.first_line = yylloc.last_line;
  yylloc.first_column = yylloc.last_column;

  /* Process numbers.  */
  if (isdigit (c))
    {
      yylval = c - '0';
      ++yylloc.last_column;
      while (isdigit (c = getchar ()))
        {
          ++yylloc.last_column;
          yylval = yylval * 10 + c - '0';
        }
      ungetc (c, stdin);
      return NUM;
    }

  /* Return end-of-input.  */
  if (c == EOF)
    return 0;

  /* Return a single char, and update location.  */
  if (c == '\n')
    {
      ++yylloc.last_line;
      yylloc.last_column = 0;
    }
  else
    ++yylloc.last_column;
  return c;
}
```

Basically, this lexical analyzer uses the same processing methods as the earlier version: it skips blanks and tabs, and reads numbers or single-character tokens. In addition, it updates `yylloc`, the global variable (of type `YYLTYPE`) containing the token's location.

Now, each time this function returns a token, the parser has the token's number as well as its semantic value, and its location in the text. The last needed change is to initialize `yylloc`, such as in the controlling function:

```
int
main (void)
{
  yylloc.first_line = yylloc.last_line = 1;
  yylloc.first_column = yylloc.last_column = 0;
  return yyparse ();
}
```

Remember that computing locations is not a matter of syntax. Every character in every valid input, comment, literal string, etc. must be associated to a location update.

2.5 Multifunction Calculator: `mfcalc`

Now that the basics of Bison have been discussed, it is time to move on to a more advanced problem. The above calculators provided only five functions, '+', '-', '*', '/' and '^'. It would be nice to have a calculator that provides other mathematical functions such as `sin`, `cos`, etc.

It is easy to add new operators to the infix calculator as long as they are only single-character literals. The lexical analyzer `yylex` passes back all nonnumber characters as tokens, so new grammar rules suffice for adding a new operator. But we want something more flexible: built-in functions whose syntax has this form:

> *function_name* (*argument*)

At the same time, we will add memory to the calculator, by allowing you to create named variables, store values in them, and use them later. Here is a sample session with the multifunction calculator:

```
$ mfcalc
pi = 3.141592653589
3.1415926536
sin(pi)
0.0000000000
alpha = beta1 = 2.3
2.3000000000
alpha
2.3000000000
ln(alpha)
0.8329091229
```

```
exp(ln(beta1))
2.3000000000
$
```

Note that multiple assignment and nested function calls are permitted.

2.5.1 Declarations for `mfcalc`

Here are the C and Bison declarations for the multifunction calculator.

```
%{
  #include <math.h>  /* For math functions, cos(), sin(), etc.  */
  #include "calc.h"  /* Contains definition of 'symrec'.  */
  int yylex (void);
  void yyerror (char const *);
%}
%union {
  double   val;   /* For returning numbers.  */
  symrec *tptr;   /* For returning symbol-table pointers.  */
}
%token <val>  NUM        /* Simple double-precision number.  */
%token <tptr> VAR FNCT   /* Variable and Function.  */
%type  <val>  exp

%right '='
%left '-' '+'
%left '*' '/'
%left NEG     /* negation--unary minus */
%right '^'    /* exponentiation */
%% /* The grammar follows.  */
```

The above grammar introduces only two new features of the Bison language.
These features allow semantic values to have various data types (see Section 3.5.2
[More Than One Value Type], page 49).

The `%union` declaration specifies the entire list of possible types; this is instead
of defining YYSTYPE. The allowable types are now double-floats (for `exp` and
NUM) and pointers to entries in the symbol table. (See Section 3.7.3 [The Collection
of Value Types], page 58.)

Since values can now have various types, it is necessary to associate a type
with each grammar symbol whose semantic value is used. These symbols are NUM,
VAR, FNCT, and `exp`. Their declarations are augmented with information about
their data type (placed between angle brackets).

The Bison construct `%type` is used for declaring nonterminal symbols, just
as `%token` is used for declaring token types. We have not used `%type` before
because nonterminal symbols are normally declared implicitly by the rules that
define them. But `exp` must be declared explicitly so we can specify its value type.
(See Section 3.7.4 [Nonterminal Symbols], page 58.)

2.5.2 Grammar Rules for `mfcalc`

Here are the grammar rules for the multifunction calculator. Most of them are copied directly from `calc`; three rules, those that mention VAR or FNCT, are new.

```
input:   /* empty */
       | input line
     ;

line:
         '\n'
       | exp '\n'    { printf ("\t%.10g\n", $1); }
       | error '\n' { yyerrok;                   }
     ;

exp:     NUM                   { $$ = $1;                          }
       | VAR                   { $$ = $1->value.var;               }
       | VAR '=' exp           { $$ = $3; $1->value.var = $3;      }
       | FNCT '(' exp ')'      { $$ = (*($1->value.fnctptr))($3);  }
       | exp '+' exp           { $$ = $1 + $3;                     }
       | exp '-' exp           { $$ = $1 - $3;                     }
       | exp '*' exp           { $$ = $1 * $3;                     }
       | exp '/' exp           { $$ = $1 / $3;                     }
       | '-' exp  %prec NEG    { $$ = -$2;                         }
       | exp '^' exp           { $$ = pow ($1, $3);                }
       | '(' exp ')'           { $$ = $2;                          }
     ;
/* End of grammar.  */
%%
```

2.5.3 The `mfcalc` Symbol Table

The multifunction calculator requires a symbol table to keep track of the names and meanings of variables and functions. This doesn't affect the grammar rules (except for the actions) or the Bison declarations, but it requires some additional C functions for support.

The symbol table itself consists of a linked list of records. Its definition, which is kept in the header 'calc.h', is as follows. It provides for either functions or variables to be placed in the table.

```
/* Function type.  */
typedef double (*func_t) (double);
```

```
/* Data type for links in the chain of symbols.  */
struct symrec
{
  char *name;  /* name of symbol */
  int type;      /* type of symbol: either VAR or FNCT */
  union
  {
    double var;        /* value of a VAR */
    func_t fnctptr;  /* value of a FNCT */
  } value;
  struct symrec *next;  /* link field */
};

typedef struct symrec symrec;

/* The symbol table: a chain of 'struct symrec'.  */
extern symrec *sym_table;

symrec *putsym (char const *, func_t);
symrec *getsym (char const *);
```

The new version of `main` includes a call to `init_table`, a function that initializes the symbol table. Below is the new version, along with `init_table`.

```
#include <stdio.h>

/* Called by yyparse on error.  */
void
yyerror (char const *s)
{
  printf ("%s\n", s);
}

struct init
{
  char const *fname;
  double (*fnct) (double);
};
```

```
struct init const arith_fncts[] =
{
  "sin",   sin,
  "cos",   cos,
  "atan",  atan,
  "ln",    log,
  "exp",   exp,
  "sqrt",  sqrt,
  0, 0
};

/* The symbol table: a chain of 'struct symrec'.  */
symrec *sym_table;

/* Put arithmetic functions in table.  */
void
init_table (void)
{
  int i;
  symrec *ptr;
  for (i = 0; arith_fncts[i].fname != 0; i++)
    {
      ptr = putsym (arith_fncts[i].fname, FNCT);
      ptr->value.fnctptr = arith_fncts[i].fnct;
    }
}

int
main (void)
{
  init_table ();
  return yyparse ();
}
```

By simply editing the initialization list and adding the necessary include files, you can add additional functions to the calculator.

Two important functions allow look-up and installation of symbols in the symbol table. The function putsym is passed a name and the type (VAR or FNCT) of the object to be installed. The object is linked to the front of the list, and a pointer to the object is returned. The function getsym is passed the name of the symbol to look up. If found, a pointer to that symbol is returned; otherwise zero is returned.

```
symrec *
putsym (char const *sym_name, int sym_type)
{
  symrec *ptr;
  ptr = (symrec *) malloc (sizeof (symrec));
  ptr->name = (char *) malloc (strlen (sym_name) + 1);
```

```
    strcpy (ptr->name,sym_name);
    ptr->type = sym_type;
    ptr->value.var = 0; /* Set value to 0 even if fctn.  */
    ptr->next = (struct symrec *)sym_table;
    sym_table = ptr;
    return ptr;
  }

symrec *
getsym (char const *sym_name)
{
  symrec *ptr;
  for (ptr = sym_table; ptr != (symrec *) 0;
       ptr = (symrec *)ptr->next)
    if (strcmp (ptr->name,sym_name) == 0)
      return ptr;
  return 0;
}
```

The function `yylex` must now recognize variables, numeric values, and the single-character arithmetic operators. Strings of alphanumeric characters with a leading non-digit are recognized as either variables or functions depending on what the symbol table says about them.

The string is passed to `getsym` for look up in the symbol table. If the name appears in the table, a pointer to its location and its type (VAR or FNCT) is returned to `yyparse`. If it is not already in the table, then it is installed as a VAR using `putsym`. Again, a pointer and its type (which must be VAR) is returned to `yyparse`.

No change is needed in the handling of numeric values and arithmetic operators in `yylex`.

```
#include <ctype.h>

int
yylex (void)
{
  int c;

  /* Ignore white space, get first nonwhite character.  */
  while ((c = getchar ()) == ' ' || c == '\t');

  if (c == EOF)
    return 0;
```

```
/* Char starts a number => parse the number.         */
if (c == '.' || isdigit (c))
  {
    ungetc (c, stdin);
    scanf ("%lf", &yylval.val);
    return NUM;
  }

/* Char starts an identifier => read the name.        */
if (isalpha (c))
  {
    symrec *s;
    static char *symbuf = 0;
    static int length = 0;
    int i;

    /* Initially make the buffer long enough
       for a 40-character symbol name.  */
    if (length == 0)
      length = 40, symbuf = (char *)malloc (length + 1);

    i = 0;
    do
      {
        /* If buffer is full, make it bigger.         */
        if (i == length)
          {
            length *= 2;
            symbuf = (char *) realloc (symbuf, length + 1);
          }
        /* Add this character to the buffer.          */
        symbuf[i++] = c;
        /* Get another character.                     */
        c = getchar ();
      }
    while (isalnum (c));

    ungetc (c, stdin);
    symbuf[i] = '\0';
```

```
        s = getsym (symbuf);
        if (s == 0)
          s = putsym (symbuf, VAR);
        yylval.tptr = s;
        return s->type;
      }

    /* Any other character is a token by itself.          */
    return c;
  }
```

This program is both powerful and flexible. You can easily add new functions, and it is also a simple job to modify this code to install predefined variables such as pi or e.

2.6 Exercises

1. Add some new functions from 'math.h' to the initialization list.
2. Add another array that contains constants and their values. Then modify init_table to add these constants to the symbol table. It will be easiest to give the constants type VAR.
3. Make the program report an error if the user refers to an uninitialized variable in any way except to store a value in it.

3 Bison Grammar Files

Bison takes as input a context-free grammar specification and produces a C-language function that recognizes correct instances of the grammar.

The Bison grammar input file conventionally has a name ending in '.y'. (See Chapter 9 [Invoking Bison], page 101.)

3.1 Outline of a Bison Grammar

A Bison grammar file has four main sections, shown here with the appropriate delimiters:

```
%{
    Prologue
%}

Bison declarations

%%
Grammar rules
%%

Epilogue
```

Comments enclosed in '/* ... */' may appear in any of the sections. As a GNU extension, '//' introduces a comment that continues until end of line.

3.1.1 The Prologue

The *prologue* section contains macro definitions and declarations of functions and variables that are used in the actions in the grammar rules. These are copied to the beginning of the parser file so that they precede the definition of yyparse. You can use '#include' to get the declarations from a header file. If you don't need any C declarations, you may omit the '%{' and '%}' delimiters that bracket this section.

You may have more than one prologue section, intermixed with the *Bison declarations*. This allows you to have C and Bison declarations that refer to each other. For example, the %union declaration may use types defined in a header file, and you may wish to prototype functions that take arguments of type YYSTYPE. This can be done with two prologue blocks, one before and one after the %union declaration.

```
%{
  #include <stdio.h>
  #include "ptypes.h"
%}
```

```
%union {
  long n;
  tree t;   /* tree is defined in 'ptypes.h'. */
}

%{
  static void print_token_value (FILE *, int, YYSTYPE);
  #define YYPRINT(F, N, L) print_token_value (F, N, L)
%}

...
```

3.1.2 The Bison Declarations Section

The *Bison declarations* section contains declarations that define terminal and nonterminal symbols, specify precedence, and so on. In some simple grammars you may not need any declarations. (See Section 3.7 [Bison Declarations], page 56.)

3.1.3 The Grammar Rules Section

The *grammar rules* section contains one or more Bison grammar rules, and nothing else. (See Section 3.3 [Syntax of Grammar Rules], page 47.)

There must always be at least one grammar rule, and the first '%%' (which precedes the grammar rules) may never be omitted even if it is the first thing in the file.

3.1.4 The Epilogue

The *epilogue* is copied verbatim to the end of the parser file, just as the prologue is copied to the beginning. This is the most convenient place to put anything that you want to have in the parser file that does not need to come before the definition of yyparse. For example, the definitions of yylex and yyerror often go here. Because C requires functions to be declared before being used, you often need to declare functions like yylex and yyerror in the prologue, even if you define them in the epilogue. (See Chapter 4 [Parser C-Language Interface], page 65.)

If the last section is empty, you may omit the '%%' that separates it from the grammar rules.

The Bison parser itself contains many macros and identifiers whose names start with 'yy' or 'YY', so it is a good idea to avoid using any such names (except those documented in this manual) in the epilogue of the grammar file.

3.2 Symbols, Terminal and Nonterminal

Symbols in Bison grammars represent the grammatical classifications of the language.

A *terminal symbol* (also known as a *token type*) represents a class of syntactically equivalent tokens. You use the symbol in grammar rules to mean that a token in that class is allowed. The symbol is represented in the Bison parser by a numeric code, and the `yylex` function returns a token type code to indicate what kind of token has been read. You don't need to know what the code value is; you can use the symbol to stand for it.

A *nonterminal symbol* stands for a class of syntactically equivalent groupings. The symbol name is used in writing grammar rules. By convention, it should be all lowercase.

Symbol names can contain letters, digits (not at the beginning), underscores and periods. Periods make sense only in nonterminals.

There are three ways of writing terminal symbols in the grammar:

- A *named token type* is written with an identifier, like an identifier in C. By convention, it should be all uppercase. Each such name must be defined with a Bison declaration such as `%token`. (See Section 3.7.1 [Token Type Names], page 56.)

- A *character token type* (or *literal character token*) is written in the grammar using the same syntax used in C for character constants; for example, `'+'` is a character token type. A character token type doesn't need to be declared unless you need to specify its semantic value data type (see Section 3.5.1 [Data Types of Semantic Values], page 49), associativity, or precedence (see Section 5.3 [Operator Precedence], page 75).

  By convention, a character token type is used only to represent a token that consists of that particular character. Thus, the token type `'+'` is used to represent the character '+' as a token. Nothing enforces this convention, but if you depart from it, your program will confuse other readers.

  All the usual escape sequences used in character literals in C can be used in Bison as well, but you must not use the null character as a character literal because its numeric code, zero, signifies end-of-input (see Section 4.2.1 [Calling Convention for `yylex`], page 66). Also, unlike Standard C, trigraphs have no special meaning in Bison character literals, nor is backslash-newline allowed.

- A *literal string token* is written like a C string constant; for example, `"<="` is a literal string token. A literal string token doesn't need to be declared unless you need to specify its semantic value data type (see Section 3.5.1 [Value Type], page 49), associativity, or precedence (see Section 5.3 [Precedence], page 75).

  You can associate the literal string token with a symbolic name as an alias, using the `%token` declaration (see Section 3.7.1 [Token Declarations], page 56). If you don't do that, the lexical analyzer has to retrieve the token number for the literal string token from the `yytname` table. (See Section 4.2.1 [Calling Convention], page 66.)

  Warning: literal string tokens do not work in Yacc.

  By convention, a literal string token is used only to represent a token that consists of that particular string. Thus, you should use the token type `"<="` to represent the string '<=' as a token. Bison does not enforce this convention, but if you depart from it, people who read your program will be confused.

All the escape sequences used in string literals in C can be used in Bison as well. However, unlike Standard C, trigraphs have no special meaning in Bison string literals, nor is backslash-newline allowed. A literal string token must contain two or more characters; for a token containing just one character, use a character token (see above).

How you choose to write a terminal symbol has no effect on its grammatical meaning. That depends only on where it appears in rules and on when the parser function returns that symbol.

The value returned by yylex is always one of the terminal symbols, except that a zero or negative value signifies end-of-input. Whichever way you write the token type in the grammar rules, you write it the same way in the definition of yylex. The numeric code for a character token type is simply the positive numeric code of the character, so yylex can use the identical value to generate the requisite code, though you may need to convert it to unsigned char to avoid sign-extension on hosts where char is signed. Each named token type becomes a C macro in the parser file, so yylex can use the name to stand for the code. (This is why periods don't make sense in terminal symbols.) (See Section 4.2.1 [Calling Convention for yylex], page 66.)

If yylex is defined in a separate file, you need to arrange for the token type macro definitions to be available there. Use the '-d' option when you run Bison, so that it will write these macro definitions into a separate header file 'name.tab.h' which you can include in the other source files that need it. (See Chapter 9 [Invoking Bison], page 101.)

If you want to write a grammar that is portable to any Standard C host, you must use only non-null character tokens taken from the basic execution character set of Standard C. This set consists of the ten digits, the 52 lowercase and uppercase English letters, and the characters in the following C-language string:

```
"\a\b\t\n\v\f\r !\"#%&'()*+,-./:;<=>?[\\]^_{|}~"
```

The yylex function and Bison must use a consistent character set and encoding for character tokens. For example, if you run Bison in an ASCII environment, but then compile and run the resulting program in an environment that uses an incompatible character set like EBCDIC, the resulting program may not work because the tables generated by Bison will assume ASCII numeric values for character tokens. It is standard practice for software distributions to contain C source files that were generated by Bison in an ASCII environment, so installers on platforms that are incompatible with ASCII must rebuild those files before compiling them.

The symbol error is a terminal symbol reserved for error recovery (see Chapter 6 [Error Recovery], page 85); you shouldn't use it for any other purpose. In particular, yylex should never return this value. The default value of the error token is 256, unless you explicitly assigned 256 to one of your tokens with a %token declaration.

3.3 Syntax of Grammar Rules

A Bison grammar rule has the following general form:

```
result :  components . . .
       ;
```

where *result* is the nonterminal symbol that this rule describes, and *components* are various terminal and nonterminal symbols that are put together by this rule (see Section 3.2 [Symbols], page 44).

For example:

```
exp:      exp '+' exp
       ;
```

says that two groupings of type `exp`, with a '+' token in between, can be combined into a larger grouping of type `exp`.

White space in rules is significant only to separate symbols. You can add extra white space as you wish.

Scattered among the components can be *actions* that determine the semantics of the rule. An action looks like this:

```
{ C statements }
```

Usually there is only one action and it follows the components. (See Section 3.5.3 [Actions], page 49.)

Multiple rules for the same *result* can be written separately or can be joined with the vertical-bar character '|' as follows:

```
result :      rule1-components . . .
       |  rule2-components . . .
          . . .
       ;
```

They are still considered distinct rules even when joined in this way.

If *components* in a rule is empty, it means that *result* can match the empty string. For example, here is how to define a comma-separated sequence of zero or more `exp` groupings:

```
expseq:   /* empty */
        | expseq1
        ;

expseq1: exp
        | expseq1 ',' exp
        ;
```

It is customary to write a comment '/* empty */' in each rule with no components.

3.4 Recursive Rules

A rule is called *recursive* when its *result* nonterminal appears also on its right hand side. Nearly all Bison grammars need to use recursion, because that is the only way to define a sequence of any number of a particular thing. Consider this recursive definition of a comma-separated sequence of one or more expressions:

```
expseq1:  exp
        | expseq1 ',' exp
        ;
```

Since the recursive use of expseq1 is the symbol farthest to the left on the right hand side, we call this *left recursion*. By contrast, here the same construct is defined using *right recursion*:

```
expseq1:  exp
        | exp ',' expseq1
        ;
```

Though any kind of sequence can be defined using either left recursion or right recursion, you should always use left recursion, because it can parse a sequence of any number of elements with bounded stack space. Right recursion uses up space on the Bison stack in proportion to the number of elements in the sequence, because all the elements must be shifted onto the stack before the rule can be applied even once. (See Chapter 5 [The Bison Parser Algorithm], page 73, for further explanation of this.)

Indirect or *mutual recursion* occurs when the result of the rule does not appear directly on its right hand side, but does appear in rules for other nonterminals which do appear on its right hand side.

For example:

```
expr:     primary
        | primary '+' primary
        ;

primary:  constant
        | '(' expr ')'
        ;
```

defines two mutually-recursive nonterminals, since each refers to the other.

3.5 Defining Language Semantics

The grammar rules for a language determine only the syntax. The semantics is determined by the semantic values associated with various tokens and groupings, and by the actions taken when various groupings are recognized.

For example, the calculator calculates properly because the value associated with each expression is the proper number; it adds properly because the action for the grouping '*x* + *y*' is to add the numbers associated with *x* and *y*.

3.5.1 Data Types of Semantic Values

In a simple program it may be sufficient to use the same data type for the semantic values of all language constructs. This was true in the RPN and infix calculator
examples. (See Section 2.1 [Reverse Polish Notation Calculator], page 23.)

Bison's default is to use type `int` for all semantic values. To specify some other
type, define YYSTYPE as a macro, like this:

```
#define YYSTYPE double
```

This macro definition must go in the prologue of the grammar file. (See Section 3.1
[Outline of a Bison Grammar], page 43.)

3.5.2 More Than One Value Type

In most programs, you will need different data types for different kinds of tokens
and groupings. For example, a numeric constant may need type `int` or `long`,
while a string constant needs type `char *`, and an identifier might need a pointer
to an entry in the symbol table.

To use more than one data type for semantic values in one parser, Bison requires
you to do two things:

• Specify the entire collection of possible data types, with the %union Bison
  declaration. (See Section 3.7.3 [The Collection of Value Types], page 58.)

• Choose one of those types for each symbol (terminal or nonterminal) for which
  semantic values are used. This is done for tokens with the %token Bison declaration (see Section 3.7.1 [Token Type Names], page 56) and for groupings
  with the %type Bison declaration (see Section 3.7.4 [Nonterminal Symbols],
  page 58).

3.5.3 Actions

An action accompanies a syntactic rule and contains C code to be executed
each time an instance of that rule is recognized. The task of most actions is to
compute a semantic value for the grouping built by the rule from the semantic
values associated with tokens or smaller groupings.

An action consists of C statements surrounded by braces, much like a compound
statement in C. An action can contain any sequence of C statements. Bison does
not look for trigraphs, though, so if your C code uses trigraphs you should ensure
that they do not affect the nesting of braces or the boundaries of comments, strings,
or character literals.

An action can be placed at any position in the rule; it is executed at that position.
Most rules have just one action at the end of the rule, following all the components.
Actions in the middle of a rule are tricky and used only for special purposes. (See
Section 3.5.5 [Actions in Mid-Rule], page 51.)

The C code in an action can refer to the semantic values of the components
matched by the rule with the construct $n, which stands for the value of the nth

component. The semantic value for the grouping being constructed is $$. (Bison translates both of these constructs into array element references when it copies the actions into the parser file.)

Here is a typical example:

```
exp:    ...
        | exp '+' exp
            { $$ = $1 + $3; }
```

This rule constructs an exp from two smaller exp groupings connected by a plus-sign token. In the action, $1 and $3 refer to the semantic values of the two component exp groupings, which are the first and third symbols on the right hand side of the rule. The sum is stored into $$ so that it becomes the semantic value of the addition-expression just recognized by the rule. If there were a useful semantic value associated with the '+' token, it could be referred to as $2.

Note that the vertical-bar character '|' is really a rule separator, and actions are attached to a single rule. This is a difference with tools like Flex, for which '|' stands for either "or", or "the same action as that of the next rule". In the following example, the action is triggered only when 'b' is found:

```
a-or-b: 'a'|'b'    { a_or_b_found = 1; };
```

If you don't specify an action for a rule, Bison supplies a default: $$ = $1. Thus, the value of the first symbol in the rule becomes the value of the whole rule. Of course, the default action is valid only if the two data types match. There is no meaningful default action for an empty rule; every empty rule must have an explicit action unless the rule's value does not matter.

$n with n zero or negative is allowed for reference to tokens and groupings on the stack *before* those that match the current rule. This is a very risky practice, and to use it reliably you must be certain of the context in which the rule is applied. Here is a case in which you can use this reliably:

```
foo:    expr bar '+' expr    { ... }
        | expr bar '-' expr    { ... }
        ;

bar:    /* empty */
        { previous_expr = $0; }
        ;
```

As long as bar is used only in the fashion shown here, $0 always refers to the expr which precedes bar in the definition of foo.

3.5.4 Data Types of Values in Actions

If you have chosen a single data type for semantic values, the $$ and $n constructs always have that data type.

If you have used %union to specify a variety of data types, then you must declare a choice among these types for each terminal or nonterminal symbol that can have a semantic value. Then each time you use $$ or $n, its data type is determined by which symbol it refers to in the rule. In this example:

```
exp:    ...
    | exp '+' exp
        { $$ = $1 + $3; }
```

$1 and $3 refer to instances of exp, so they all have the data type declared for the nonterminal symbol exp. If $2 were used, it would have the data type declared for the terminal symbol '+', whatever that might be.

Alternatively, you can specify the data type when you refer to the value, by inserting '<*type*>' after the '$' at the beginning of the reference. For example, if you have defined types as shown here:

```
%union {
    int itype;
    double dtype;
}
```

then you can write $<itype>1 to refer to the first subunit of the rule as an integer, or $<dtype>1 to refer to it as a double.

3.5.5 Actions in Mid-Rule

Occasionally it is useful to put an action in the middle of a rule. These actions are written just like usual end-of-rule actions, but they are executed before the parser even recognizes the components that come after the action.

A mid-rule action may refer to the components preceding it using $n, but it may not refer to subsequent components because it is run before they are parsed.

The mid-rule action itself counts as one of the components of the rule. This makes a difference when there is another action later in the same rule (and usually there is another at the end); you have to count the actions along with the symbols when working out which number n to use in $n.

The mid-rule action can also have a semantic value. The action can set its value with an assignment to $$, and actions later in the rule can refer to the value using $n. Since there is no symbol to name the action, there is no way to declare a data type for the value in advance, so you must use the '$<...>n' construct to specify a data type each time you refer to this value.

There is no way to set the value of the entire rule with a mid-rule action, because assignments to $$ do not have that effect. The only way to set the value for the entire rule is with an ordinary action at the end of the rule.

Here is an example from a hypothetical compiler, handling a let statement that looks like 'let (*variable*) *statement*' and serves to create a variable named *variable* temporarily for the duration of *statement*. To parse this construct, we must put *variable* into the symbol table while *statement* is parsed, then remove it afterward. Here is how it is done:

```
stmt:    LET '(' var ')'
                   { $<context>$ = push_context ();
                     declare_variable ($3); }
         stmt    { $$ = $6;
                   pop_context ($<context>5); }
```

As soon as 'let (*variable*)' has been recognized, the first action is run. It saves a copy of the current semantic context (the list of accessible variables) as its semantic value, using alternative context in the data type union. Then it calls declare_ variable to add the new variable to that list. Once the first action is finished, the embedded statement stmt can be parsed. Note that the mid-rule action is component number 5, so the 'stmt' is component number 6.

After the embedded statement is parsed, its semantic value becomes the value of the entire let statement. Then the semantic value from the earlier action is used to restore the prior list of variables. This removes the temporary let variable from the list so that it won't appear to exist while the rest of the program is parsed.

Taking action before a rule is completely recognized often leads to conflicts since the parser must commit to a parse in order to execute the action. For example, the following two rules, without mid-rule actions, can coexist in a working parser because the parser can shift the open-brace token and look at what follows before deciding whether there is a declaration or not:

```
compound: '{' declarations statements '}'
        | '{' statements '}'
        ;
```

But when we add a mid-rule action as follows, the rules become nonfunctional:

```
compound: { prepare_for_local_variables (); }
            '{' declarations statements '}'
        | '{' statements '}'
        ;
```

Now the parser is forced to decide whether to run the mid-rule action when it has read no farther than the open-brace. In other words, it must commit to using one rule or the other without sufficient information to do it correctly. (The open-brace token is what is called the *look-ahead* token at this time, since the parser is still deciding what to do about it. See Section 5.1 [Look-Ahead Tokens], page 73.)

You might think that you could correct the problem by putting identical actions into the two rules, like this:

```
compound: { prepare_for_local_variables (); }
            '{' declarations statements '}'
        | { prepare_for_local_variables (); }
            '{' statements '}'
        ;
```

But this does not help, because Bison does not realize that the two actions are identical (Bison never tries to understand the C code in an action).

If the grammar is such that a declaration can be distinguished from a statement by the first token (which is true in C), then one solution that does work is to put the action after the open-brace, like this:

```
compound: '{' { prepare_for_local_variables (); }
            declarations statements '}'
        | '{' statements '}'
        ;
```

Now the first token of the following declaration or statement, which would in any case tell Bison which rule to use, can still do so.

Another solution is to bury the action inside a nonterminal symbol which serves as a subroutine:

```
subroutine: /* empty */
              { prepare_for_local_variables (); }
          ;


compound: subroutine
            '{' declarations statements '}'
        | subroutine
            '{' statements '}'
        ;
```

Now Bison can execute the action in the rule for subroutine without deciding which rule for compound it will eventually use. Note that the action is now at the end of its rule. Any mid-rule action can be converted to an end-of-rule action in this way; this is what Bison actually does to implement mid-rule actions.

3.6 Tracking Locations

Though grammar rules and semantic actions are enough to write a fully functional parser, it can be useful to process some additional information, especially symbol locations.

The way locations are handled is defined by providing a data type, and actions to take when rules are matched.

3.6.1 Data Type of Locations

Defining a data type for locations is much simpler than for semantic values, since all tokens and groupings always use the same type.

The type for locations is specified by defining a macro called YYLTYPE. When YYLTYPE is not defined, Bison uses a default structure type with four members:

```
typedef struct YYLTYPE
{
  int first_line;
  int first_column;
```

```
        int last_line;
        int last_column;
    } YYLTYPE;
```

3.6.2 Actions and Locations

Actions are not only useful for defining language semantics, but also for describing the behavior of the output parser with locations.

The most obvious way to build locations of syntactic groupings is very similar
to the way semantic values are computed. In a given rule, several constructs can
be used to access the locations of the elements being matched. The location of the
nth component of the right hand side is @n, while the location of the left hand side
grouping is @$.

Here is a basic example using the default data type for locations:

```
exp:    ...
    | exp '/' exp
        {
            @$.first_column = @1.first_column;
            @$.first_line = @1.first_line;
            @$.last_column = @3.last_column;
            @$.last_line = @3.last_line;
            if ($3)
              $$ = $1 / $3;
            else
              {
                $$ = 1;
                printf("Division by zero, l%d,c%d-l%d,c%d",
                        @3.first_line, @3.first_column,
                        @3.last_line, @3.last_column);
              }
        }
```

As for semantic values, there is a default action for locations that is run each
time a rule is matched. It sets the beginning of @$ to the beginning of the first
symbol, and the end of @$ to the end of the last symbol.

With this default action, the location tracking can be fully automatic. The example above can be rewritten this way:

```
exp:    ...
    | exp '/' exp
        {
            if ($3)
                $$ = $1 / $3;
            else
                {
                    $$ = 1;
                    printf("Division by zero, l%d,c%d-l%d,c%d",
                            @3.first_line, @3.first_column,
                            @3.last_line, @3.last_column);
                }
        }
```

3.6.3 Default Action for Locations

Actually, actions are not the best place to compute locations. Since locations are much more general than semantic values, there is room in the output parser to redefine the default action to take for each rule. The YYLLOC_DEFAULT macro is invoked each time a rule is matched, before the associated action is run. It is also invoked while processing a syntax error, to compute the error's location.

Most of the time, this macro is general enough to suppress location dedicated code from semantic actions.

The YYLLOC_DEFAULT macro takes three parameters. The first one is the location of the grouping (the result of the computation). When a rule is matched, the second parameter is an array holding locations of all elements on the right hand side of the rule being matched, and the third parameter is the size of the rule's right hand side. When processing a syntax error, the second parameter is an array holding locations of the symbols that were discarded during error processing, and the third parameter is the number of discarded symbols.

By default, YYLLOC_DEFAULT is defined this way for simple LALR(1) parsers:

```
# define YYLLOC_DEFAULT(Current, Rhs, N) \
    ((Current).first_line   = (Rhs)[1].first_line, \
     (Current).first_column = (Rhs)[1].first_column, \
     (Current).last_line     = (Rhs)[N].last_line, \
     (Current).last_column   = (Rhs)[N].last_column)
```

and like this for GLR parsers:

```
# define YYLLOC_DEFAULT(yyCurrent, yyRhs, YYN) \
    ((yyCurrent).first_line = YYRHSLOC(yyRhs, 1).first_line, \
     (yyCurrent).first_column = YYRHSLOC(yyRhs, 1).first_column, \
     (yyCurrent).last_line = YYRHSLOC(yyRhs, YYN).last_line, \
     (yyCurrent).last_column  = YYRHSLOC(yyRhs, YYN).last_column)
```

When defining YYLLOC_DEFAULT, you should consider that:

- All arguments are free of side-effects. However, only the first one (the result) should be modified by `YYLLOC_DEFAULT`.

- For consistency with semantic actions, valid indexes for the location array range from 1 to *n*.

- Your macro should parenthesize its arguments, if need be, since the actual arguments may not be surrounded by parentheses. Also, your macro should expand to something that can be used as a single statement when it is followed by a semicolon.

3.7 Bison Declarations

The *Bison declarations* section of a Bison grammar defines the symbols used in formulating the grammar and the data types of semantic values. (See Section 3.2 [Symbols], page 44.)

All token type names (but not single-character literal tokens such as `'+'` and `'*'`) must be declared. Nonterminal symbols must be declared if you need to specify which data type to use for the semantic value. (See Section 3.5.2 [More Than One Value Type], page 49.)

The first rule in the file also specifies the start-symbol, by default. If you want some other symbol to be the start-symbol, you must declare it explicitly. (See Section 1.1 [Languages and Context-Free Grammars], page 13.)

3.7.1 Token Type Names

The basic way to declare a token type name (terminal symbol) is as follows:

```
%token name
```

Bison will convert this into a `#define` directive in the parser, so that the function `yylex` (if it is in this file) can use the name *name* to stand for this token type's code.

Alternatively, you can use `%left`, `%right`, or `%nonassoc` instead of `%token`, if you wish to specify associativity and precedence. (See Section 3.7.2 [Operator Precedence], page 57.)

You can explicitly specify the numeric code for a token type by entering an integer value in the field immediately following the token name:

```
%token NUM 300
```

It is generally best, however, to let Bison choose the numeric codes for all token types. Bison will automatically select codes that don't conflict with each other or with normal characters.

In the event that the stack type is a union, you must augment the `%token` or other token declaration to include, delimited by angle brackets, the alternative data type. (See Section 3.5.2 [More Than One Value Type], page 49.)

For example:

```
%union {                    /* define stack type */
  double val;
  symrec *tptr;
}
%token <val> NUM       /* define token NUM and its type */
```

You can associate a literal string token with a token type name by writing the literal string at the end of a `%token` declaration that declares the name. For example:

```
%token arrow "=>"
```

A grammar for the C language might specify these names with equivalent literal string tokens:

```
%token  <operator>  OR        "||"
%token  <operator>  LE 134    "<="
%left   OR   "<="
```

Once you equate the literal string and the token name, you can use them interchangeably in further declarations or grammar rules. The `yylex` function can use the token name or the literal string to obtain the token type code number. (See Section 4.2.1 [Calling Convention], page 66.)

3.7.2 Operator Precedence

Use the `%left`, `%right` or `%nonassoc` declaration to simultaneously declare a token and specify its precedence and associativity. These are called *precedence declarations*. (See Section 5.3 [Operator Precedence], page 75.)

The syntax of a precedence declaration is the same as that of `%token`: either

```
%left symbols...
```

or

```
%left <type> symbols...
```

Any of these declarations do indeed serve the purposes of `%token`. But they also specify the associativity and relative precedence for all the *symbols*:

- The associativity of an operator *op* determines how repeated uses of the operator nest: whether 'x *op* y *op* z' is parsed by grouping x with y first or by grouping y with z first. `%left` specifies left associativity (grouping x with y first) and `%right` specifies right associativity (grouping y with z first). `%nonassoc` specifies no associativity, which means that 'x *op* y *op* z' is considered a syntax error.

- The precedence of an operator determines how it nests with other operators. All the tokens declared in a single precedence declaration have equal precedence and nest together according to their associativity. When two tokens declared in different precedence declarations associate, the one declared later has the higher precedence and is grouped first.

3.7.3 The Collection of Value Types

The %union declaration specifies the entire collection of possible data types for semantic values. The keyword %union is followed by a pair of braces containing the same thing that goes inside a union in C.

For example:

```
%union {
  double val;
  symrec *tptr;
}
```

This says that the two alternative types are double and symrec *. They are given names val and tptr; these names are used in the %token and %type declarations to pick one of the types for a terminal or nonterminal symbol. (See Section 3.7.4 [Nonterminal Symbols], page 58.)

As an extension to POSIX, a tag is allowed after the union. For example:

```
%union value {
  double val;
  symrec *tptr;
}
```

specifies the union tag value, so the corresponding C type is union value. If you do not specify a tag, it defaults to YYSTYPE.

Note that unlike making a union declaration in C, you need not write a semi-colon after the closing brace.

3.7.4 Nonterminal Symbols

When you use %union to specify multiple value types, you must declare the value type of each nonterminal symbol for which values are used. This is done with a %type declaration, like this:

```
%type <type> nonterminal ...
```

Here *nonterminal* is the name of a nonterminal symbol, and *type* is the name given in the %union to the alternative that you want. (See Section 3.7.3 [The Collection of Value Types], page 58.) You can give any number of nonterminal symbols in the same %type declaration, if they have the same value type. Use spaces to separate the symbol names.

You can also declare the value type of a terminal symbol. To do this, use the same *<type>* construction in a declaration for the terminal symbol. All forms of token declarations allow *<type>*.

3.7.5 Freeing Discarded Symbols

Some symbols can be discarded by the parser, typically during error recovery. (See Chapter 6 [Error Recovery], page 85.) Basically, during error recovery, em-barrassing symbols already pushed on the stack, and embarrassing tokens coming from the rest of the file are thrown away until the parser falls on its feet. If these symbols convey heap based information, this memory is lost. While this behavior is tolerable for batch parsers, such as in compilers, it is unacceptable for parsers that can potentially "never end", such as shells or implementations of communication protocols.

The %destructor directive allows for the definition of code that is called when a symbol is thrown away.

%destructor { *code* } *symbols*   Directive

Declare that the *code* must be invoked for each of the *symbols* that will be discarded by the parser. The *code* should use $$ to designate the semantic value associated to the *symbols*. The additional parser parameters are also available. (See Section 4.1 [The Parser Function yyparse], page 65.)

Warning: as of Bison 1.875, this feature is still considered experimental, as there was not enough user feedback. Be aware that the syntax might be changed in later versions.

For instance:

```
%union
{
    char *string;
}
%token <string> STRING
%type  <string> string
%destructor { free ($$); } STRING string
```

guarantees that when a STRING or a string will be discarded, its associated memory will be freed.

Note that in the future, Bison might also consider that right hand side members that are not mentioned in the action can be destroyed. For instance, in:

```
comment: "/*" STRING "*/";
```

the parser is entitled to destroy the semantic value of the string. Of course, this will not apply to the default action; compare:

```
typeless: string;  // $$ = $1 does not apply; $1 is destroyed.
typefull: string;  // $$ = $1 applies, $1 is not destroyed.
```

3.7.6 Suppressing Conflict Warnings

Bison normally warns if there are any conflicts in the grammar (see Section 5.2 [Shift/Reduce Conflicts], page 74), but most real grammars have harmless shift/reduce conflicts which are resolved in a predictable way and would be difficult to eliminate. It is desirable to suppress the warning about these conflicts unless the number of conflicts changes. You can do this with the %expect declaration.

The declaration looks like this:

```
%expect n
```

Here *n* is a decimal integer. The declaration says there should be no warning if
there are *n* shift/reduce conflicts and no reduce/reduce conflicts. The usual warning
is given if there are either more or fewer shift/reduce conflicts, or any reduce/reduce
conflicts.

In general, using `%expect` involves these steps:

- Compile your grammar without `%expect`. Use the '`-v`' option to get a verbose list of where the conflicts occur. Bison will also print the number of
  conflicts.

- Check each of the conflicts to make sure that Bison's default resolution is what
  you really want. If not, rewrite the grammar and go back to the beginning.

- Add an `%expect` declaration, copying the number *n* from the number that
  Bison printed.

Now Bison will stop annoying you if you do not change the number of conflicts, but it will warn you again if changes in the grammar result in more or fewer
conflicts.

3.7.7 The Start-Symbol

Bison assumes by default that the start-symbol for the grammar is the first nonterminal specified in the grammar specification section. The programmer may over-
ride this restriction with the `%start` declaration as follows:

```
%start symbol
```

3.7.8 A Pure (Reentrant) Parser

A *reentrant* program is one that does not alter in the course of execution; in
other words, it consists entirely of *pure* (read-only) code. Reentrancy is important
whenever asynchronous execution is possible; for example, a nonreentrant program
may not be safe to call from a signal handler. In systems with multiple threads of
control, a nonreentrant program must be called only within interlocks.

Normally, Bison generates a parser that is not reentrant. This is suitable for
most uses, and it permits compatibility with Yacc. (The standard Yacc interfaces
are inherently nonreentrant, because they use statically allocated variables for communication with `yylex`, including `yylval` and `yylloc`.)

Alternatively, you can generate a pure, reentrant parser. The Bison declaration
`%pure-parser` says that you want the parser to be reentrant. It looks like this:

```
%pure-parser
```

The result is that the communication variables `yylval` and `yylloc` become
local variables in `yyparse`, and a different calling convention is used for the lexical analyzer function `yylex`. (See Section 4.2.4 [Calling Conventions for Pure
Parsers], page 68.) The variable `yynerrs` also becomes local in `yyparse`. (See
Section 4.3 [The Error Reporting Function `yyerror`], page 69.) The convention
for calling `yyparse` itself is unchanged.

Whether the parser is pure has nothing to do with the grammar rules. You can generate either a pure parser or a nonreentrant parser from any valid grammar.

3.7.9 Bison Declaration Summary

Here is a summary of the declarations used to define a grammar:

%union   Directive
Declare the collection of data types that semantic values may have. (See Section 3.7.3 [The Collection of Value Types], page 58.)

%token   Directive
Declare a terminal symbol (token type name) with no precedence or associativity specified. (See Section 3.7.1 [Token Type Names], page 56.)

%right   Directive
Declare a terminal symbol (token type name) that is right-associative. (See Section 3.7.2 [Operator Precedence], page 57.)

%left   Directive
Declare a terminal symbol (token type name) that is left-associative. (See Section 3.7.2 [Operator Precedence], page 57.)

%nonassoc   Directive
Declare a terminal symbol (token type name) that is nonassociative–using it in a way that would be associative is a syntax error. (See Section 3.7.2 [Operator Precedence], page 57.)

%type   Directive
Declare the type of semantic values for a nonterminal symbol. (See Section 3.7.4 [Nonterminal Symbols], page 58.)

%start   Directive
Specify the grammar's start-symbol. (See Section 3.7.7 [The Start-Symbol], page 60.)

%expect   Directive
Declare the expected number of shift/reduce conflicts. (See Section 3.7.6 [Suppressing Conflict Warnings], page 59.)

In order to change the behavior of Bison, use the following directives:

%debug   Directive
In the parser file, define the macro YYDEBUG to 1 if it is not already defined, so that the debugging facilities are compiled. (See Section 8.2 [Tracing Your Parser], page 97.)

%defines   Directive
> Write an extra output file containing macro definitions for the token type names
> defined in the grammar and the semantic value type YYSTYPE, as well as a few
> extern variable declarations.
>
> If the parser output file is named 'name.c' then this file is named 'name.h'.
>
> This output file is essential if you wish to put the definition of yylex in a
> separate source file, because yylex needs to be able to refer to token type codes
> and the variable yylval. (See Section 4.2.2 [Semantic Values of Tokens],
> page 67.)

%destructor   Directive
> Specify how the parser should reclaim the memory associated to discarded sym-
> bols. (See Section 3.7.5 [Freeing Discarded Symbols], page 58.)

%file-prefix="*prefix***"**   Directive
> Specify a prefix to use for all Bison output file names. The names are chosen as
> if the input file were named 'prefix.y'.

%locations   Directive
> Generate the code processing the locations. (See Section 4.4 [Special Features
> for Use in Actions], page 71.) This mode is enabled as soon as the grammar
> uses the special '@n' tokens, but even if your grammar does not make use of
> the mode, using '%locations' still allows for more accurate syntax error
> messages.

%name-prefix="*prefix***"**   Directive
> Rename the external symbols used in the parser so that they start with *prefix*
> instead of 'yy'. The precise list of symbols renamed is yyparse, yylex,
> yyerror, yynerrs, yylval, yylloc, yychar, yydebug, and possibly
> yylloc. For example, if you use '%name-prefix="c_"', the names be-
> come c_parse, c_lex, and so on. (See Section 3.8 [Multiple Parsers in the
> Same Program], page 64.)

%no-parser   Directive
> Do not include any C code in the parser file; generate tables only. The parser
> file contains just #define directives and static variable declarations.
>
> This option also tells Bison to write the C code for the grammar actions into
> a file named 'filename.act', in the form of a brace-surrounded body fit for a
> switch statement.

%no-lines   Directive
> Don't generate any #line preprocessor commands in the parser file. Ordinar-
> ily Bison writes these commands in the parser file so that the C compiler and
> debuggers will associate errors and object code with your source file (the gram-
> mar file). This directive causes them to associate errors with the parser file,
> treating it as an independent source file in its own right.

%output="*filename*"   Directive

Specify the *filename* for the parser file.

%pure-parser   Directive

Request a pure (reentrant) parser program. (See Section 3.7.8 [A Pure (Reentrant) Parser], page 60.)

%token-table   Directive

Generate an array of token names in the parser file. The name of the array is `yytname`; `yytname[i]` is the name of the token whose internal Bison token code number is *i*. The first three elements of `yytname` correspond to the predefined tokens `"$end"`, `"error"`, and `"$undefined"`; after these come the symbols defined in the grammar file.

For single-character literal tokens and literal string tokens, the name in the table includes the single-quote or double-quote characters. For example, `"'+'"` is a single-character literal and `"\"<=\""` is a literal string token. All the characters of the literal string token appear verbatim in the string found in the table; even double-quote characters are not escaped. For example, if the token consists of three characters '`*"*`', its string in `yytname` contains '`"*"*"`'. (In C, that would be written as `"\"*\"*\""`).

When you specify `%token-table`, Bison also generates macro definitions for macros YYNTOKENS, YYNNTS, YYNRULES, and YYNSTATES:

YYNTOKENS
> The highest token number, plus one

YYNNTS   The number of nonterminal symbols

YYNRULES
> The number of grammar rules

YYNSTATES
> The number of parser states (see Section 5.5 [Parser States], page 78)

%verbose   Directive

Write an extra output file containing verbose descriptions of the parser states and what is done for each type of look-ahead token in that state. (See Section 8.1 [Understanding Your Parser], page 91.)

%yacc   Directive

Pretend the option '`--yacc`' was given, i.e., imitate Yacc, including its naming conventions. (See Section 9.1 [Bison Options], page 101.)

3.8 Multiple Parsers in the Same Program

Most programs that use Bison parse only one language and therefore contain only one Bison parser. But what if you want to parse more than one language with the same program? Then you need to avoid a name conflict between different definitions of `yyparse`, `yylval`, and so on.

The easy way to do this is to use the option '-p *prefix*'. (See Chapter 9 [Invoking Bison], page 101.) This renames the interface functions and variables of the Bison parser to start with *prefix* instead of 'yy'. You can use this to give each parser distinct names that do not conflict.

The precise list of symbols renamed is `yyparse`, `yylex`, `yyerror`, `yynerrs`, `yylval`, `yylloc`, `yychar` and `yydebug`. For example, if you use '-p c', the names become `cparse`, `clex`, and so on.

None of the other variables and macros associated with Bison are renamed. These others are not global; there is no conflict if the same name is used in different parsers. For example, `YYSTYPE` is not renamed, but defining this in different ways in different parsers does not cause any trouble. (See Section 3.5.1 [Data Types of Semantic Values], page 49.)

The '-p' option works by adding macro definitions to the beginning of the parser source file, defining `yyparse` as *prefix*`parse`, and so on. This effectively substitutes one name for the other throughout the entire parser file.

4 Parser C-Language Interface

The Bison parser is actually a C function named `yyparse`. Here we describe the interface conventions of `yyparse` and the other functions that it needs to use.

Keep in mind that the parser uses many C identifiers starting with 'yy' and 'YY' for internal purposes. If you use such an identifier (aside from those in this manual) in an action or in the epilogue in the grammar file, you are likely to run into trouble.

4.1 The Parser Function `yyparse`

You call the function `yyparse` to cause parsing to occur. This function reads tokens, executes actions, and ultimately returns when it encounters end-of-input or an unrecoverable syntax error. You can also write an action which directs `yyparse` to return immediately without reading further.

int **yyparse** (void)   Function
> The value returned by `yyparse` is 0 if parsing was successful (return is due to end-of-input).
>
> The value is 1 if parsing failed (return is due to a syntax error).

In an action, you can cause immediate return from `yyparse` by using these macros:

YYACCEPT   Macro
> Return immediately with value 0 (to report success).

YYABORT   Macro
> Return immediately with value 1 (to report failure).

If you use a reentrant parser, you can optionally pass additional parameter information to it in a reentrant way. To do so, use the declaration `%parse-param`:

%**parse-param** {*argument-declaration*}   Directive
> Declare that an argument declared by `argument-declaration` is an additional `yyparse` argument. The *argument-declaration* is used when declaring functions or prototypes. The last identifier in *argument-declaration* must be the argument name.

Here's an example. Write this in the parser:

```
%parse-param {int *nastiness}
%parse-param {int *randomness}
```
Then call the parser like this:

```
{
    int nastiness, randomness;
    ...  /* Store proper data in nastiness and randomness.  */
```

```
    value = yyparse (&nastiness, &randomness);
    ...
}
```

In the grammar actions, use expressions like this to refer to the data:

```
exp: ...    { ...; *randomness += 1; ... }
```

4.2 The Lexical Analyzer Function `yylex`

The *lexical analyzer* function, `yylex`, recognizes tokens from the input stream and returns them to the parser. Bison does not create this function automatically; you must write it so that `yyparse` can call it. The function is sometimes referred to as a lexical scanner.

In simple programs, `yylex` is often defined at the end of the Bison grammar file. If `yylex` is defined in a separate source file, you need to arrange for the token type macro definitions to be available there. To do this, use the '-d' option when you run Bison. It will write these macro definitions into a separate header file '*name*.tab.h' which you can include in any other source files that need it. (See Chapter 9 [Invoking Bison], page 101.)

4.2.1 Calling Convention for `yylex`

The value that `yylex` returns must be the positive numeric code for the type of token it has just found; a zero or negative value signifies end-of-input.

When a token is referred to in the grammar rules by a name, that name in the parser file becomes a C macro whose definition is the proper numeric code for that token type. So `yylex` can use the name to indicate that type. (See Section 3.2 [Symbols], page 44.)

When a token is referred to in the grammar rules by a character literal, the numeric code for that character is also the code for the token type. So `yylex` can simply return that character code, possibly converted to `unsigned char` to avoid sign-extension. The null character must not be used this way, because its code is zero and that signifies end-of-input. For example:

```
int
yylex (void)
{
  ...
  if (c == EOF)     /* Detect end-of-input.  */
    return 0;
  ...
  if (c == '+' || c == '-')
    return c;       /* Assume token type for '+' is '+'.  */
  ...
  return INT;       /* Return the type of the token.  */
  ...
}
```

This interface has been designed so that the output from the `lex` utility can be used without change as the definition of `yylex`.

If the grammar uses literal string tokens, there are two ways that `yylex` can determine the token type codes for them:

- If the grammar defines symbolic token names as aliases for the literal string tokens, `yylex` can use these symbolic names like all the others it uses. In this case, the use of the literal string tokens in the grammar file has no effect on `yylex`.

- `yylex` can find the multicharacter token in the `yytname` table. The index of the token in the table is the token type's code. The name of a multicharacter token is recorded in `yytname` with a double-quote, the token's characters, and another double-quote. The token's characters are not escaped in any way; they appear verbatim in the contents of the string in the table.

Here is code for looking up a token in `yytname`, assuming that the characters of the token are stored in `token_buffer`:

```
for (i = 0; i < YYNTOKENS; i++)
  {
    if (yytname[i] != 0
        && yytname[i][0] == '"'
        && ! strncmp (yytname[i] + 1, token_buffer,
                      strlen (token_buffer))
        && yytname[i][strlen (token_buffer) + 1] == '"'
        && yytname[i][strlen (token_buffer) + 2] == 0)
      break;
  }
```

The `yytname` table is generated only if you use the `%token-table` declaration. (See Section 3.7.9 [Decl Summary], page 61.)

4.2.2 Semantic Values of Tokens

In an ordinary (nonreentrant) parser, the semantic value of the token must be stored in the global variable `yylval`. When you are using just one data type for semantic values, `yylval` has that type. Thus, if the type is `int` (the default), you might write this in `yylex`:

```
...
yylval = value;  /* Put value onto Bison stack.  */
return INT;      /* Return the type of the token.  */
...
```

When you are using multiple data types, `yylval`'s type is a union made from the `%union` declaration. (See Section 3.7.3 [The Collection of Value Types], page 58.) When you store a token's value, you must use the proper member of the union. If the `%union` declaration looks like this:

```
%union {
  int intval;
  double val;
  symrec *tptr;
}
```

then the code in `yylex` might look like this:

```
...
yylval.intval = value; /* Put value onto Bison stack.  */
return INT;            /* Return the type of the token.  */
...
```

4.2.3 Textual Locations of Tokens

If you are using the '@*n*'-feature (see Section 3.6 [Tracking Locations], page 53) in actions to keep track of the textual locations of tokens and groupings, then you must provide this information in `yylex`. The function `yyparse` expects to find the textual location of a just-parsed token in the global variable `yylloc`, so `yylex` must store the proper data in that variable.

By default, the value of `yylloc` is a structure and you need only initialize the members that are going to be used by the actions. The four members are called `first_line`, `first_column`, `last_line` and `last_column`. Note that the use of this feature makes the parser noticeably slower.

The data type of `yylloc` has the name YYLTYPE.

4.2.4 Calling Conventions for Pure Parsers

When you use the Bison declaration `%pure-parser` to request a pure, reentrant parser, the global communication variables `yylval` and `yylloc` cannot be used. (See Section 3.7.8 [A Pure (Reentrant) Parser], page 60.) In such parsers the two global variables are replaced by pointers passed as arguments to `yylex`. You must declare them as shown here, and pass the information back by storing it through those pointers.

```
int
yylex (YYSTYPE *lvalp, YYLTYPE *llocp)
{
  ...
  *lvalp = value;  /* Put value onto Bison stack.  */
  return INT;      /* Return the type of the token.  */
  ...
}
```

If the grammar file does not use the '@' constructs to refer to textual locations, then the type YYLTYPE will not be defined. In this case, omit the second argument; `yylex` will be called with only one argument.

If you wish to pass the additional parameter data to `yylex`, use `%lex-param` just like `%parse-param` (see Section 4.1 [Parser Function], page 65).

lex-param {*argument-declaration*}   Directive
Declare that `argument-declaration` is an additional `yylex` argument declaration.

For instance:

```
%parse-param {int *nastiness}
%lex-param   {int *nastiness}
%parse-param {int *randomness}
```

results in the following signature:

```
int yylex   (int *nastiness);
int yyparse (int *nastiness, int *randomness);
```

If `%pure-parser` is added:

```
int yylex   (YYSTYPE *lvalp, int *nastiness);
int yyparse (int *nastiness, int *randomness);
```

and finally, if both `%pure-parser` and `%locations` are used:

```
int yylex   (YYSTYPE *lvalp, YYLTYPE *llocp, int *nastiness);
int yyparse (int *nastiness, int *randomness);
```

4.3 The Error Reporting Function `yyerror`

The Bison parser detects a *syntax error* or *parse error* whenever it reads a token that cannot satisfy any syntax rule. An action in the grammar can also explicitly proclaim an error, using the macro YYERROR. (See Section 4.4 [Special Features for Use in Actions], page 71.)

The Bison parser expects to report the error by calling an error-reporting function named `yyerror`, which you must supply. It is called by `yyparse` whenever a syntax error is found, and it receives one argument. For a syntax error, the string is normally `"syntax error"`.

If you invoke the directive `%error-verbose` in the Bison declarations section (see Section 3.1.2 [The Bison Declarations Section], page 44), then Bison provides a more verbose and specific error message string than just plain `"syntax error"`.

The parser can detect one other kind of error: stack overflow. This error happens when the input contains constructions that are very deeply nested. It isn't likely you will encounter this, since the Bison parser extends its stack automatically up to a very large limit. But if overflow does happen, `yyparse` calls `yyerror` in the usual fashion, except that the argument string is `"parser stack overflow"`.

The following definition suffices in simple programs:

```
void
yyerror (char const *s)
{
```

```
    fprintf (stderr, "%s\n", s);
}
```

After `yyerror` returns to `yyparse`, the latter will attempt error recovery if you have written suitable error recovery grammar rules. (See Chapter 6 [Error Recovery], page 85.) If recovery is impossible, `yyparse` will immediately return 1.

Obviously, in location tracking pure parsers, `yyerror` should have an access to the current location. This is indeed the case for the GLR parsers, but not for the Yacc parser, for historical reasons. I.e., if '`%locations %pure-parser`' is passed then the prototypes for `yyerror` are:

```
void yyerror (char const *msg);                    /* Yacc parsers.  */
void yyerror (YYLTYPE *locp, char const *msg);  /* GLR parsers.   */
```

If '`%parse-param {int *nastiness}`' is used, then:

```
void yyerror (int *nastiness, char const *msg);  /* Yacc parsers.  */
void yyerror (int *nastiness, char const *msg);  /* GLR parsers.   */
```

Finally, GLR and Yacc parsers share the same `yyerror` calling convention for absolutely pure parsers, i.e., when the calling convention of `yylex` *and* the calling convention of `%pure-parser` are pure. I.e.:

```
/* Location tracking.  */
%locations
/* Pure yylex.  */
%pure-parser
%lex-param   {int *nastiness}
/* Pure yyparse.  */
%parse-param {int *nastiness}
%parse-param {int *randomness}
```

results in the following signatures for all the parser kinds:

```
int yylex (YYSTYPE *lvalp, YYLTYPE *llocp, int *nastiness);
int yyparse (int *nastiness, int *randomness);
void yyerror (YYLTYPE *locp,
              int *nastiness, int *randomness,
              char const *msg);
```

The prototypes are only indications of how the code produced by Bison uses `yyerror`. Bison-generated code always ignores the returned value, so `yyerror` can return any type, including `void`. Also, `yyerror` can be a variadic function; that is why the message is always passed last.

Traditionally `yyerror` returns an `int` that is always ignored, but this is purely for historical reasons, and `void` is preferable since it more accurately describes the return type for `yyerror`.

The variable `yynerrs` contains the number of syntax errors encountered so far. Normally this variable is global; but if you request a pure parser (see Section 3.7.8 [A Pure (Reentrant) Parser], page 60) then it is a local variable that only the actions can access.

4.4 Special Features for Use in Actions

Here is a table of Bison constructs, variables and macros that are useful in actions.

$$ Variable

Acts like a variable that contains the semantic value for the grouping made by the current rule. (See Section 3.5.3 [Actions], page 49.)

$*n*   Variable

Acts like a variable that contains the semantic value for the *n*th component of the current rule. (See Section 3.5.3 [Actions], page 49.)

$<*typealt*>$ Variable

Like $$ but specifies alternative *typealt* in the union specified by the %union declaration. (See Section 3.5.4 [Data Types of Values in Actions], page 50.)

$<*typealt*>*n*   Variable

Like $*n* but specifies alternative *typealt* in the union specified by the %union declaration. (See Section 3.5.4 [Data Types of Values in Actions], page 50.)

YYABORT;   Macro

Return immediately from yyparse, indicating failure. (See Section 4.1 [The Parser Function yyparse], page 65.)

YYACCEPT;   Macro

Return immediately from yyparse, indicating success. (See Section 4.1 [The Parser Function yyparse], page 65.)

YYBACKUP (*token, value*);   Macro

Unshift a token. This macro is allowed only for rules that reduce a single value, and only when there is no look-ahead token. It is also disallowed in GLR parsers. It installs a look-ahead token with token type *token* and semantic value *value*, then it discards the value that was going to be reduced by this rule.

If the macro is used when it is not valid, such as when there is a look-ahead token already, then it reports a syntax error with a message 'cannot back up' and performs ordinary error recovery.

In either case, the rest of the action is not executed.

YYEMPTY   Macro

Value stored in yychar when there is no look-ahead token.

YYERROR;   Macro

Cause an immediate syntax error. This statement initiates error recovery just as if the parser itself had detected an error; however, it does not call yyerror,

and does not print any message. If you want to print an error message, call
`yyerror` explicitly before the 'YYERROR;' statement. (See Chapter 6 [Error
Recovery], page 85.)

YYRECOVERING   Macro

This macro stands for an expression that has the value 1 when the parser is
recovering from a syntax error, and 0 the rest of the time. (See Chapter 6 [Error
Recovery], page 85.)

yychar   Variable

Variable containing the current look-ahead token. (In a pure parser, this is actually a local variable within `yyparse`.) When there is no look-ahead token,
the value YYEMPTY is stored in the variable. (See Section 5.1 [Look-Ahead
Tokens], page 73.)

yyclearin;   Macro

Discard the current look-ahead token. This is useful primarily in error rules.
(See Chapter 6 [Error Recovery], page 85.)

yyerrok;   Macro

Resume generating error messages immediately for subsequent syntax errors.
This is useful primarily in error rules. (See Chapter 6 [Error Recovery],
page 85.)

@$ Value

Acts like a structure variable containing information on the textual location of
the grouping made by the current rule. (See Section 3.6 [Tracking Locations],
page 53.)

@n   Value

Acts like a structure variable containing information on the textual location of
the nth component of the current rule. See Section 3.6 [Tracking Locations],
page 53.

5 The Bison Parser Algorithm

As Bison reads tokens, it pushes them onto a stack along with their semantic values. The stack is called the *parser stack*. Pushing a token is traditionally called *shifting*.

For example, suppose the infix calculator has read '1 + 5 *', with a '3' to come. The stack will have four elements, one for each token that was shifted.

But the stack does not always have an element for each token read. When the last *n* tokens and groupings shifted match the components of a grammar rule, they can be combined according to that rule. This is called *reduction*. Those tokens and groupings are replaced on the stack by a single grouping whose symbol is the result (left hand side) of that rule. Running the rule's action is part of the process of reduction, because this is what computes the semantic value of the resulting grouping.

For example, if the infix calculator's parser stack contains this:

```
1 + 5 * 3
```

and the next input token is a newline character, then the last three elements can be reduced to 15 via the rule:

```
expr: expr '*' expr;
```

Then the stack contains just these three elements:

```
1 + 15
```

At this point, another reduction can be made, resulting in the single value 16. Then the newline token can be shifted.

The parser tries, by shifts and reductions, to reduce the entire input down to a single grouping whose symbol is the grammar's start-symbol. (See Section 1.1 [Languages and Context-Free Grammars], page 13.)

This kind of parser is known in the literature as a bottom-up parser.

5.1 Look-Ahead Tokens

The Bison parser does *not* always reduce immediately when the last *n* tokens and groupings match a rule. This is because such a simple strategy is inadequate to handle most languages. Instead, when a reduction is possible, the parser sometimes "looks ahead" at the next token in order to decide what to do.

When a token is read, it is not immediately shifted; first it becomes the *look-ahead token*, which is not on the stack. Now the parser can perform one or more reductions of tokens and groupings on the stack, while the look-ahead token remains off to the side. When no more reductions should take place, the look-ahead token is shifted onto the stack. This does not mean that all possible reductions have been done; depending on the token type of the look-ahead token, some rules may choose to delay their application.

Here is a simple case where look-ahead is needed. These three rules define expressions that contain binary addition operators and postfix unary factorial operators ('!'), and allow parentheses for grouping:

```
expr:     term '+' expr
        | term
        ;

term:     '(' expr ')'
        | term '!'
        | NUMBER
        ;
```

Suppose that the tokens '1 + 2' have been read and shifted; what should be done? If the following token is ')', then the first three tokens must be reduced to form an `expr`. This is the only valid course, because shifting the ')' would produce a sequence of symbols `term ')'`, and no rule allows this.

If the following token is '!', then it must be shifted immediately so that '2 !' can be reduced to make a `term`. If instead the parser were to reduce before shifting, '1 + 2' would become an `expr`. It would then be impossible to shift the '!' because doing so would produce on the stack the sequence of symbols `expr '!'`. No rule allows that sequence.

The current look-ahead token is stored in the variable `yychar`. (See Section 4.4 [Special Features for Use in Actions], page 71.)

5.2 Shift/Reduce Conflicts

Suppose we are parsing a language which has if-then and if-then-else statements, with a pair of rules like this:

```
if_stmt:
            IF expr THEN stmt
        | IF expr THEN stmt ELSE stmt
        ;
```

Here we assume that `IF`, `THEN` and `ELSE` are terminal symbols for specific keyword tokens.

When the `ELSE` token is read and becomes the look-ahead token, the contents of the stack (assuming the input is valid) are just right for reduction by the first rule. But it is also legitimate to shift the `ELSE`, because that would lead to eventual reduction by the second rule.

This situation, where either a shift or a reduction would be valid, is called a *shift/reduce conflict*. Bison is designed to resolve these conflicts by choosing to shift, unless otherwise directed by operator precedence declarations. To see the reason for this, let's contrast it with the other alternative.

Since the parser prefers to shift the `ELSE`, the result is to attach the else-clause to the innermost if-statement, making these two inputs equivalent:

```
if x then if y then win (); else lose;
```

```
if x then do; if y then win (); else lose; end;
```

But if the parser chose to reduce when possible rather than shift, the result would be to attach the else-clause to the outermost if-statement, making these two inputs equivalent:

```
if x then if y then win (); else lose;
```

```
if x then do; if y then win (); end; else lose;
```

The conflict exists because the grammar as written is ambiguous: either parsing of the simple nested if-statement is legitimate. The established convention is to resolve these ambiguities by attaching the else-clause to the innermost if-statement. This is what Bison accomplishes by choosing to shift rather than reduce. (It ideally would be cleaner to write an unambiguous grammar, but that is very hard to do in this case.) This particular ambiguity was first encountered in the specifications of Algol 60 and is called the "dangling else" ambiguity.

To avoid warnings from Bison about predictable, legitimate shift/reduce conflicts, use the %expect *n* declaration. There will be no warning as long as the number of shift/reduce conflicts is exactly *n*. (See Section 3.7.6 [Suppressing Conflict Warnings], page 59.)

The definition of if_stmt above is solely to blame for the conflict, but the conflict does not actually appear absent additional rules. Here is a complete Bison input file that actually manifests the conflict:

```
%token IF THEN ELSE variable
%%
stmt:       expr
          | if_stmt
          ;

if_stmt:
            IF expr THEN stmt
          | IF expr THEN stmt ELSE stmt
          ;

expr:       variable
          ;
```

5.3 Operator Precedence

Another situation where shift/reduce conflicts appear is in arithmetic expressions. Here shifting is not always the preferred resolution; the Bison declarations for operator precedence allow you to specify when to shift and when to reduce.

5.3.1 When Precedence is Needed

Consider the following ambiguous grammar fragment (ambiguous because the input '1 - 2 * 3' can be parsed in two different ways):

```
expr:      expr '-' expr
         | expr '*' expr
         | expr '<' expr
         | '(' expr ')'
         ...
         ;
```

Suppose the parser has seen the tokens '1', '-' and '2'; should it reduce them via the rule for the subtraction operator? It depends on the next token. Of course, if the next token is ')', we must reduce; shifting is invalid because no single rule can reduce the token sequence '- 2)' or anything starting with that. But if the next token is '*' or '<', we have a choice: either shifting or reducing would allow the parse to complete, but each would produce different results.

To decide which one Bison should choose, we must consider the results. If the next operator token *op* is shifted, then it must be reduced first in order to permit another opportunity to reduce the difference. The result is (in effect) '1 - (2 *op* 3)'. On the other hand, if the subtraction is reduced before shifting *op*, the result is '(1 - 2) *op* 3'. Clearly, then, the choice of shift or reduce should depend on the relative precedence of the operators '-' and *op*: '*' should be shifted first, but not '<'.

What about input such as '1 - 2 - 5'; should this be '(1 - 2) - 5' or should it be '1 - (2 - 5)'? For most operators we prefer the former, which is called *left association*. The latter alternative, *right association*, is desirable for assignment operators. The choice of left or right association is a matter of whether the parser chooses to shift or reduce when the stack contains '1 - 2' and the look-ahead token is '-': shifting produces right associativity.

5.3.2 Specifying Operator Precedence

Bison allows you to specify these choices with the operator precedence declarations %left and %right. Each such declaration contains a list of tokens, which are operators whose precedence and associativity are being declared. The %left declaration makes all those operators left-associative and the %right declaration makes them right-associative. A third alternative is %nonassoc, which declares that it is a syntax error to find the same operator twice "in a row".

The relative precedence of different operators is controlled by the order in which they are declared. The first %left or %right declaration in the file declares the operators whose precedence is lowest, the next such declaration declares the operators whose precedence is a little higher, and so on.

5.3.3 Precedence Examples

In our example, we would want the following declarations:

```
%left '<'
%left '-'
%left '*'
```

In a more complete example, which would support additional operators, we would declare them in groups of equal precedence. For example, `'+'` is declared with `'-'`:

```
%left '<' '>' '=' NE LE GE
%left '+' '-'
%left '*' '/'
```

(Here NE and so on stand for the operators for "not equal", "less than or equal" and "greater than or equal". We assume that these tokens are more than one character long and therefore are represented by names, not character literals.)

5.3.4 How Precedence Works

The first effect of the precedence declarations is to assign precedence levels to the terminal symbols declared. The second effect is to assign precedence levels to certain rules: each rule gets its precedence from the last terminal symbol mentioned in its components. You can also specify explicitly the precedence of a rule. (See Section 5.4 [Context-Dependent Precedence], page 77.)

Finally, conflicts are resolved by comparing the precedence of the rule being considered with that of the look-ahead token. If the token's precedence is higher, the choice is to shift. If the rule's precedence is higher, the choice is to reduce. If they have equal precedence, the choice is made based on the associativity of that precedence level. The verbose output file made by '-v' (see Chapter 9 [Invoking Bison], page 101) says how each conflict was resolved.

Not all rules and not all tokens have precedence. If either the rule or the look-ahead token has no precedence, then the default is to shift.

5.4 Context-Dependent Precedence

Often the precedence of an operator depends on the context. This sounds outlandish at first, but it is really very common. For example, a minus sign typically has a very high precedence as a unary operator, and a somewhat lower precedence (lower than multiplication) as a binary operator.

The Bison precedence declarations, %left, %right and %nonassoc, can only be used once for a given token; so a token has only one precedence declared in this way. For context-dependent precedence, you need to use an additional mechanism: the %prec modifier for rules.

The `%prec` modifier declares the precedence of a particular rule by specifying a terminal symbol whose precedence should be used for that rule. It's not necessary for that symbol to appear otherwise in the rule. The modifier's syntax is:

```
%prec terminal-symbol
```

and it is written after the components of the rule. Its effect is to assign the rule the precedence of *terminal-symbol*, overriding the precedence that would be deduced for it in the ordinary way. The altered rule precedence then affects how conflicts involving that rule are resolved. (See Section 5.3 [Operator Precedence], page 75.)

Here is how `%prec` solves the problem of the unary minus. First, declare a precedence for a fictitious terminal symbol named UMINUS. There are no tokens of this type, but the symbol serves to stand for its precedence:

```
...
%left '+' '-'
%left '*'
%left UMINUS
```

Now the precedence of UMINUS can be used in specific rules:

```
exp:    ...
        | exp '-' exp
        ...
        | '-' exp %prec UMINUS
```

5.5 Parser States

The function `yyparse` is implemented using a finite-state machine. The values pushed on the parser stack are not simply token type codes; they represent the entire sequence of terminal and nonterminal symbols at or near the top of the stack. The current state collects all the information about previous input that is relevant to deciding what to do next.

Each time a look-ahead token is read, the current parser state together with the type of look-ahead token are looked up in a table. This table entry can say, "Shift the look-ahead token". In this case, it also specifies the new parser state, which is pushed onto the top of the parser stack. Or it can say, "Reduce using rule number *n*". This means that a certain number of tokens or groupings are taken off the top of the stack, and replaced by one grouping. In other words, that number of states are popped from the stack, and one new state is pushed.

There is one other alternative: the table can say that the look-ahead token is erroneous in the current state. This causes error processing to begin. (See Chapter 6 [Error Recovery], page 85.)

5.6 Reduce/Reduce Conflicts

A reduce/reduce conflict occurs if there are two or more rules that apply to the same sequence of input. This usually indicates a serious error in the grammar.

For example, here is an erroneous attempt to define a sequence of zero or more
`word` groupings.

```
sequence: /* empty */
                { printf ("empty sequence\n"); }
        | maybeword
        | sequence word
                { printf ("added word %s\n", $2); }
        ;

maybeword: /* empty */
                { printf ("empty maybeword\n"); }
        | word
                { printf ("single word %s\n", $1); }
        ;
```

The error is an ambiguity: there is more than one way to parse a single `word` into a
`sequence`. It could be reduced to a `maybeword` and then into a `sequence` via
the second rule. Alternatively, nothing-at-all could be reduced into a `sequence`
via the first rule, and this could be combined with the `word` using the third rule for
`sequence`.

There is also more than one way to reduce nothing-at-all into a `sequence`.
This can be done directly via the first rule, or indirectly via `maybeword` and then
the second rule.

You might think that this is a distinction without a difference, because it does
not change whether any particular input is valid or not. But it does affect which
actions are run. One parsing order runs the second rule's action; the other runs
the first rule's action and the third rule's action. In this example, the output of the
program changes.

Bison resolves a reduce/reduce conflict by choosing to use the rule that appears first in the grammar, but it is very risky to rely on this. Every reduce/reduce
conflict must be studied and usually eliminated. Here is the proper way to define
`sequence`:

```
sequence: /* empty */
                { printf ("empty sequence\n"); }
        | sequence word
                { printf ("added word %s\n", $2); }
        ;
```

Here is another common error that yields a reduce/reduce conflict:

```
sequence: /* empty */
        | sequence words
        | sequence redirects
        ;

words:    /* empty */
```

```
          | words word
          ;


redirects:/* empty */
          | redirects redirect
          ;
```

The intention here is to define a sequence which can contain either word or redirect groupings. The individual definitions of sequence, words and redirects are error-free, but the three together make a subtle ambiguity: even an empty input can be parsed in an infinite number of ways!

Consider: nothing-at-all could be a words. Or it could be two words in a row, or three, or any number. It could equally well be a redirects, or two, or any number. Or it could be a words followed by three redirects and another words. And so on.

Here are two ways to correct these rules. First, to make it a single level of sequence:

```
sequence: /* empty */
          | sequence word
          | sequence redirect
          ;
```

Second, to prevent either a words or a redirects from being empty:

```
sequence: /* empty */
          | sequence words
          | sequence redirects
          ;


words:    word
          | words word
          ;


redirects:redirect
          | redirects redirect
          ;
```

5.7 Mysterious Reduce/Reduce Conflicts

Sometimes reduce/reduce conflicts can occur that don't look warranted. Here is an example:

```
%token ID

%%
def:    param_spec return_spec ','
        ;
param_spec:
            type
        |   name_list ':' type
        ;
return_spec:
            type
        |   name ':' type
        ;
type:       ID
        ;
name:       ID
        ;
name_list:
            name
        |   name ',' name_list
        ;
```

It would seem that this grammar can be parsed with only a single token of look-ahead: when a `param_spec` is being read, an `ID` is a `name` if a comma or colon follows, or a `type` if another `ID` follows. In other words, this grammar is LR(1).

However, Bison, like most parser generators, cannot actually handle all LR(1) grammars. In this grammar, two contexts, one after an `ID` at the beginning of a `param_spec` and the other at the beginning of a `return_spec`, are similar enough that Bison assumes they are the same. They appear similar because the same set of rules would be active—the rule for reducing to a `name` and that for reducing to a `type`. Bison is unable to determine at that stage of processing that the rules would require different look-ahead tokens in the two contexts, so it makes a single parser state for both. Combining the two contexts causes a conflict later. In parser terminology, this occurrence means that the grammar is not LALR(1).

In general, it is better to fix deficiencies than to document them. But this partic-ular deficiency is intrinsically hard to fix; parser generators that can handle LR(1) grammars are hard to write and tend to produce parsers that are very large. In practice, Bison is more useful as it is now.

When the problem arises, you can often fix it by identifying the two parser states that are being confused, and adding something to make them look distinct. In the above example, adding one rule to `return_spec` as follows makes the problem go away:

```
%token BOGUS
...
%%
...
return_spec:
            type
    |   name ':' type
    /* This rule is never used.  */
    |   ID BOGUS
    ;
```

This corrects the problem because it introduces the possibility of an additional active rule in the context after the ID at the beginning of return_spec. This rule is not active in the corresponding context in a param_spec, so the two contexts receive distinct parser states. As long as the token BOGUS is never generated by yylex, the added rule cannot alter the way actual input is parsed.

In this particular example, there is another way to solve the problem: rewrite the rule for return_spec to use ID directly instead of via name. This also causes the two confusing contexts to have different sets of active rules, because the one for return_spec activates the altered rule for return_spec rather than the one for name.

```
param_spec:
            type
    |   name_list ':' type
    ;
return_spec:
            type
    |   ID ':' type
    ;
```

5.8 Generalized LR (GLR) Parsing

Bison produces *deterministic* parsers that choose uniquely when to reduce and which reduction to apply based on a summary of the preceding input and on one extra token of look-ahead. As a result, normal Bison handles a proper subset of the family of context-free languages. Ambiguous grammars, since they have strings with more than one possible sequence of reductions, cannot have deterministic parsers in this sense. The same is true of languages that require more than one symbol of look-ahead, since the parser lacks the information necessary to make a decision at the point it must be made in a shift/reduce parser. Finally, as previously mentioned (see Section 5.7 [Mystery Conflicts], page 80), there are languages where Bison's particular choice of how to summarize the input seen so far loses necessary information.

When you use the '%glr-parser' declaration in your grammar file, Bison generates a parser that uses a different algorithm, called Generalized LR (or GLR).

A Bison GLR parser uses the same basic algorithm for parsing as an ordinary Bison parser, but behaves differently in cases where there is a shift/reduce conflict that has not been resolved by precedence rules (see Section 5.3 [Precedence], page 75) or a reduce/reduce conflict. When a GLR parser encounters such a situation, it effectively *splits* into several parsers, one for each possible shift or reduction. These parsers then proceed as usual, consuming tokens in lock-step. Some of the stacks may encounter other conflicts and split further, with the result that instead of a sequence of states, a Bison GLR parsing stack is in effect a tree of states.

In effect, each stack represents a guess as to what the proper parse is. Additional input may indicate that a guess was wrong, in which case the appropriate stack silently disappears. Otherwise, the semantic actions generated in each stack are saved, rather than being executed immediately. When a stack disappears, its saved semantic actions never get executed. When a reduction causes two stacks to become equivalent, their sets of semantic actions are both saved with the state that results from the reduction. We say that two stacks are equivalent when they both represent the same sequence of states and each pair of corresponding states represents a grammar symbol that produces the same segment of the input token stream.

Whenever the parser makes a transition from having multiple states to having one, it reverts to the normal LALR(1) parsing algorithm, after resolving and executing the saved-up actions. At this transition, some of the states on the stack will have semantic values that are sets (actually multisets) of possible actions. The parser tries to pick one of the actions by first finding one whose rule has the highest dynamic precedence, as set by the '`%dprec`' declaration. If the alternative actions are not ordered by precedence, but the same merging function is declared for both rules by the '`%merge`' declaration, Bison resolves and evaluates both and then calls the merge function on the result. Otherwise, it reports an ambiguity.

It is possible to use a data structure for the GLR parsing tree that permits the processing of any LALR(1) grammar in linear time (in the size of the input), any unambiguous (not necessarily LALR(1)) grammar in quadratic worst-case time, and any general (possibly ambiguous) context-free grammar in cubic worst-case time. However, Bison currently uses a simpler data structure that requires time proportional to the length of the input times the maximum number of stacks required for any prefix of the input. Thus, particularly ambiguous or nondeterministic grammars can require exponential time and space to process. Such badly behaved examples, however, are not generally of practical interest. Usually, nondeterminism in a grammar is local–the parser is "in doubt" only for a few tokens at a time. Therefore, the current data structure should generally be adequate. On LALR(1) portions of a grammar, in particular, it is only slightly slower than with the default Bison parser.

For a more detailed exposition of GLR parsers, please see: Elizabeth Scott, Adrian Johnstone and Shamsa Sadaf Hussain, *Tomita-Style Generalised* LR *Parsers* (2000-12-24), Royal Holloway, University of London, Department of Computer Science, TR-00-12, `http://www.cs.rhul.ac.uk/research/languages/publications/`.

5.9 Stack Overflow, and How to Avoid it

The Bison parser stack can overflow if too many tokens are shifted and not reduced. When this happens, the parser function `yyparse` returns a nonzero value, pausing only to call `yyerror` to report the overflow.

Because Bison parsers have growing stacks, hitting the upper limit usually results from using a right recursion instead of a left recursion. (See Section 3.4 [Recursive Rules], page 48.)

By defining the macro `YYMAXDEPTH`, you can control how deep the parser stack can become before a stack overflow occurs. Define the macro with a value that is an integer. This value is the maximum number of tokens that can be shifted (and not reduced) before overflow. It must be a constant expression whose value is known at compile time.

The stack space allowed is not necessarily allocated. If you specify a large value for `YYMAXDEPTH`, the parser actually allocates a small stack at first, and then makes it bigger by stages as needed. This increasing allocation happens automatically and silently. Therefore, you do not need to make `YYMAXDEPTH` painfully small merely to save space for ordinary inputs that do not need much stack.

The default value of `YYMAXDEPTH`, if you do not define it, is 10000.

You can control how much stack is allocated initially by defining the macro `YYINITDEPTH`. This value too must be a compile-time constant integer. The default is 200.

Because of semantic differences between C and C++, the LALR(1) parsers in C produced by Bison and compiled as C++ cannot grow. In this precise case (compiling a C parser as C++) you should row `YYINITDEPTH`. In the near future, a C++ output will be provided which addresses this issue.

6 Error Recovery

It is not usually acceptable to have a program terminate on a syntax error. For example, a compiler should recover sufficiently to parse the rest of the input file and check it for errors; a calculator should accept another expression.

In a simple interactive command parser where each input is one line, it may be sufficient to allow `yyparse` to return 1 on error and have the caller ignore the rest of the input line when that happens (and then call `yyparse` again). But this is inadequate for a compiler, because it forgets all the syntactic context leading up to the error. A syntax error deep within a function in the compiler input should not cause the compiler to treat the following line like the beginning of a source file.

You can define how to recover from a syntax error by writing rules to recognize the special token `error`. This is a terminal symbol that is always defined (you need not declare it) and reserved for error handling. The Bison parser generates an `error` token whenever a syntax error happens. If you have provided a rule to recognize this token in the current context, the parse can continue.

For example:

```
stmnts:  /* empty string */
        | stmnts '\n'
        | stmnts exp '\n'
        | stmnts error '\n'
```

The fourth rule in this example says that an error followed by a newline makes a valid addition to any `stmnts`.

What happens if a syntax error occurs in the middle of an `exp`? The error recovery rule, interpreted strictly, applies to the precise sequence of a `stmnts`: an `error` and a newline. If an error occurs in the middle of an `exp`, there will probably be some additional tokens and subexpressions on the stack after the last `stmnts`, and there will be tokens to read before the next newline. So the rule is not applicable in the ordinary way.

But Bison can force the situation to fit the rule, by discarding part of the semantic context and part of the input. First it discards states and objects from the stack until it gets back to a state in which the `error` token is acceptable. (This means that the subexpressions already parsed are discarded, back to the last complete `stmnts`.) At this point the `error` token can be shifted. Then, if the old look-ahead token is not acceptable to be shifted next, the parser reads tokens and discards them until it finds a token which is acceptable. In this example, Bison reads and discards input until the next newline so that the fourth rule can apply. Note that discarded symbols are possible sources of memory leaks. See Section 3.7.5 [Freeing Discarded Symbols], page 58, for a means to reclaim this memory.

The choice of error rules in the grammar is a choice of strategies for error recovery. A simple and useful strategy is simply to skip the rest of the current input line or current statement if an error is detected:

```
stmnt: error ';'  /* On error, skip until ';' is read.  */
```

It is also useful to recover to the matching close-delimiter of an opening-delimiter that has already been parsed. Otherwise the close-delimiter will probably appear to be unmatched, generating another, spurious error message:

```
primary:  '(' expr ')'
       |  '(' error ')'
       ...
       ;
```

Error recovery strategies are necessarily guesses. When these guesses are wrong, one syntax error often leads to another. In the above example, the error recovery rule guesses that an error is due to bad input within one `stmnt`. Suppose that actually, a spurious semicolon is inserted in the middle of a valid `stmnt`. After the error recovery rule recovers from the first error, another syntax error will be found immediately, since the text following the spurious semicolon is also an invalid `stmnt`.

To prevent an outpouring of error messages, the parser will not output an error message for another syntax error that happens shortly after the first; only after three consecutive input tokens have been successfully shifted will error messages resume.

Note that rules which accept the `error` token may have actions, just as any other rules can.

You can make error messages resume immediately by using the macro `yyerrok` in an action. If you do this in the error rule's action, no error messages will be suppressed. This macro requires no arguments; '`yyerrok;`' is a valid C statement.

The previous look-ahead token is reanalyzed immediately after an error. If this is unacceptable, then the macro `yyclearin` may be used to clear this token. Write the statement '`yyclearin;`' in the error rule's action.

For example, suppose that on a syntax error, an error handling routine is called that advances the input stream to some point where parsing should once again commence. The next symbol returned by the lexical scanner is probably correct. The previous look-ahead token ought to be discarded with '`yyclearin;`'.

The macro `YYRECOVERING` stands for an expression that has the value 1 when the parser is recovering from a syntax error and 0 the rest of the time. A value of 1 indicates that error messages for new syntax errors are currently being suppressed.

7 Handling Context-Dependencies

The Bison paradigm is to parse tokens first, then group them into larger syntactic units. In many languages, the meaning of a token is affected by its context. Although this violates the Bison paradigm, certain techniques (known as *kludges*) may enable you to write Bison parsers for such languages.

(Actually, *kludge* means any technique that gets its job done but is neither clean nor robust.)

7.1 Semantic Info in Token Types

The C language has a context-dependency: the way an identifier is used depends on what its current meaning is. For example, consider this:

```
foo (x);
```

This looks like a function call statement, but if `foo` is a typedef name, then this is actually a declaration of `x`. How can a Bison parser for C decide how to parse this input?

The method used in GNU C is to have two different token types, `IDENTIFIER` and `TYPENAME`. When `yylex` finds an identifier, it looks up the current declaration of the identifier in order to decide which token type to return: `TYPENAME` if the identifier is declared as a typedef, `IDENTIFIER` otherwise.

The grammar rules can then express the context-dependency by the choice of token type to recognize. `IDENTIFIER` is accepted as an expression, but `TYPENAME` is not. `TYPENAME` can start a declaration, but `IDENTIFIER` cannot. In contexts where the meaning of the identifier is *not* significant, such as in declarations that can shadow a typedef name, either `TYPENAME` or `IDENTIFIER` is accepted—there is one rule for each of the two token types.

This technique is simple to use if the decision of which kinds of identifiers to allow is made at a place close to where the identifier is parsed. But in C this is not always so: C allows a declaration to redeclare a typedef name provided an explicit type has been specified earlier:

```
typedef int foo, bar, lose;
static foo (bar);         /* redeclare bar as static variable */
static int foo (lose);    /* redeclare foo as function */
```

Unfortunately, the name being declared is separated from the declaration construct itself by a complicated syntactic structure–the "declarator".

As a result, part of the Bison parser for C needs to be duplicated, with all the nonterminal names changed: once for parsing a declaration in which a typedef name can be redefined, and once for parsing a declaration in which it can't be redefined. Here is a part of the duplication, with actions omitted for brevity:

```
initdcl:
        declarator maybeasm '='
        init
```

```
      | declarator maybeasm
      ;


notype_initdcl:
          notype_declarator maybeasm '='
          init
      | notype_declarator maybeasm
      ;
```

Here `initdcl` can redeclare a typedef name, but `notype_initdcl` cannot. The distinction between `declarator` and `notype_declarator` is the same sort of thing.

There is some similarity between this technique and a *lexical tie-in* (described in the next section), in that information that alters the lexical analysis is changed during parsing by other parts of the program. The difference is that here, the information is global, and is used for other purposes in the program. A true lexical tie-in has a special-purpose flag controlled by the syntactic context.

7.2 Lexical Tie-Ins

One way to handle context-dependency is the *lexical tie-in*: a flag that is set by Bison actions, whose purpose is to alter the way tokens are parsed.

For example, suppose we have a language vaguely like C, but with a special construct 'hex (*hex-expr*)'. After the keyword `hex` comes an expression in parentheses in which all integers are hexadecimal. In particular, the token 'a1b' must be treated as an integer rather than as an identifier if it appears in that context. Here is how you can do it:

```
%{
  int hexflag;
  int yylex (void);
  void yyerror (char const *);
%}
%%
...
expr:   IDENTIFIER
      | constant
      | HEX '('
              { hexflag = 1; }
        expr ')'
              { hexflag = 0;
                $$ = $4; }
      | expr '+' expr
              { $$ = make_sum ($1, $3); }
      ...
      ;
```

```
constant:
        INTEGER
      | STRING
      ;
```

Here we assume that `yylex` looks at the value of `hexflag`; when it is nonzero, all integers are parsed in hexadecimal, and tokens starting with letters are parsed as integers if possible.

The declaration of `hexflag` shown in the prologue of the parser file is needed to make it accessible to the actions. (See Section 3.1.1 [The Prologue], page 43.) You must also write the code in `yylex` to obey the flag.

7.3 Lexical Tie-ins and Error Recovery

Lexical tie-ins make strict demands on any error recovery rules you have. (See Chapter 6 [Error Recovery], page 85.)

The reason for this is that the purpose of an error recovery rule is to abort the parsing of one construct and resume in some larger construct. For example, in C-like languages, a typical error recovery rule is to skip tokens until the next semi-colon, and then start a new statement, like this:

```
stmt:    expr ';'
       | IF '(' expr ')' stmt { ... }
       ...
       error ';'
               { hexflag = 0; }
       ;
```

If there is a syntax error in the middle of a 'hex (*expr*)' construct, this error rule will apply. The action for the completed 'hex (*expr*)' will never run. So `hexflag` would remain set for the full remainder of the input, or until the next `hex` keyword, causing identifiers to be misinterpreted as integers.

To avoid this problem, the error recovery rule itself clears `hexflag`.

There may also be an error recovery rule that works within expressions. For example, there could be a rule that applies within parentheses and skips to the close-parenthesis:

```
expr:    ...
       | '(' expr ')'
               { $$ = $2; }
       | '(' error ')'
       ...
```

If this rule acts within the `hex` construct, it is not going to abort that construct (since it applies to an inner level of parentheses within the construct). Therefore, it should not clear the flag. The rest of the `hex` construct should be parsed with the flag still in effect.

What if there is an error recovery rule that might abort out of the hex construct or might not, depending on circumstances? There is no way you can write the action to determine whether a hex construct is being aborted or not. So if you are using a lexical tie-in, you had better make sure your error recovery rules are not of this kind. Each rule must be such that you can be certain it either always will or always won't have to clear the flag.

8 Debugging Your Parser

Developing a parser can be a challenge, especially if you don't understand the algorithm. (See Chapter 5 [The Bison Parser Algorithm], page 73.) Even so, sometimes a detailed description of the automaton can help. (See Section 8.1 [Understanding Your Parser], page 91.) Tracing the execution of the parser can give some insight into why it behaves improperly. (See Section 8.2 [Tracing Your Parser], page 97.)

8.1 Understanding Your Parser

As documented elsewhere, Bison parsers are *shift/reduce automata*. (See Chapter 5 [The Bison Parser Algorithm], page 73.) Some cases (much more frequent than one would hope) require looking at this automaton to tune or fix a parser. Bison provides two different representations of it, one textual and one graphical (as a VCG file).

The textual file is generated when the options '--report' or '--verbose' are specified. (See Chapter 9 [Invoking Bison], page 101.) Its name is made by removing '.tab.c' or '.c' from the parser output file name, and adding '.output' instead. Therefore, if the input file is 'foo.y', then the parser file is called 'foo.tab.c' by default, and the verbose output file is called 'foo.output'.

The following grammar file, 'calc.y', will be used in the sequel:

```
%token NUM STR
%left '+' '-'
%left '*'
%%
exp: exp '+' exp
   | exp '-' exp
   | exp '*' exp
   | exp '/' exp
   | NUM
   ;
useless: STR;
%%
```

bison reports:

```
calc.y: warning: 1 useless nonterminal and 1 useless rule
calc.y:11.1-7: warning: useless nonterminal: useless
calc.y:11.10-12: warning: useless rule: useless: STR
calc.y: conflicts: 7 shift/reduce
```

When given '--report=state', in addition to 'calc.tab.c', it creates a file 'calc.output' with contents detailed below. The order of the output and the exact presentation might vary, but the interpretation is the same.

The first section includes details on conflicts that were solved thanks to precedence or associativity or both:

```
Conflict in state 8 between rule 2 and token '+' resolved as reduce.
Conflict in state 8 between rule 2 and token '-' resolved as reduce.
Conflict in state 8 between rule 2 and token '*' resolved as shift.
...
```

The next section lists states that still have conflicts.

```
State 8 conflicts: 1 shift/reduce
State 9 conflicts: 1 shift/reduce
State 10 conflicts: 1 shift/reduce
State 11 conflicts: 4 shift/reduce
```

The next section reports useless tokens, nonterminals and rules. Useless nonterminals and rules are removed in order to produce a smaller parser, but useless tokens are preserved, since they might be used by the scanner (note the difference between "useless" and "not used" below):

```
Useless nonterminals:
   useless


Terminals which are not used:
   STR


Useless rules:
#6      useless: STR;
```

The next section reproduces the exact grammar that Bison used:

```
Grammar


Number, Line, Rule
   0    5 $accept -> exp $end
   1    5 exp -> exp '+' exp
   2    6 exp -> exp '-' exp
   3    7 exp -> exp '*' exp
   4    8 exp -> exp '/' exp
   5    9 exp -> NUM
```

and reports the uses of the symbols:

```
Terminals, with rules where they appear


$end (0) 0
'*' (42) 3
'+' (43) 1
'-' (45) 2
'/' (47) 4
error (256)
NUM (258) 5
```

```
Nonterminals, with rules where they appear

$accept (8)
    on left: 0
exp (9)
    on left: 1 2 3 4 5, on right: 0 1 2 3 4
```

Bison then proceeds to the automaton itself, describing each state with its set of *items*, also known as *pointed rules*. Each item is a production rule together with a point (marked by '.') marking the input cursor.

```
state 0

    $accept  ->  . exp $    (rule 0)

    NUM           shift, and go to state 1

    exp           go to state 2
```

This reads as follows: "state 0 corresponds to being at the very beginning of the parsing, in the initial rule, right before the start-symbol (here, exp). When the parser returns to this state right after having reduced a rule that produced an exp, the control flow jumps to state 2. If there is no such transition on a nonterminal symbol, and the look-ahead is a NUM, then this token is shifted on the parse stack, and the control flow jumps to state 1. Any other look-ahead triggers a syntax error."

Even though the only active rule in state 0 seems to be rule 0, the report lists NUM as a look-ahead symbol because NUM can be at the beginning of any rule deriving an exp. By default Bison reports the *core* or *kernel* of the item set, but if you want to see more detail you can invoke bison with '--report=itemset' to list all the items, including those that can be derived:

```
    state 0

        $accept  ->  . exp $    (rule 0)
        exp  ->  . exp '+' exp    (rule 1)
        exp  ->  . exp '-' exp    (rule 2)
        exp  ->  . exp '*' exp    (rule 3)
        exp  ->  . exp '/' exp    (rule 4)
        exp  ->  . NUM    (rule 5)

        NUM           shift, and go to state 1

        exp           go to state 2


    state 1
```

```
exp  ->  NUM .    (rule 5)


$default     reduce using rule 5 (exp)
```

In state 1, the rule 5, 'exp: NUM;', is completed. Whatever the look-ahead ('$default'), the parser will reduce it. If the parser was coming from state 0, then after this reduction it will return to state 0, then jump to state 2 ('exp: go to state 2').

```
state 2


$accept  ->  exp . $    (rule 0)
exp  ->  exp . '+' exp    (rule 1)
exp  ->  exp . '-' exp    (rule 2)
exp  ->  exp . '*' exp    (rule 3)
exp  ->  exp . '/' exp    (rule 4)


$              shift, and go to state 3
'+'            shift, and go to state 4
'-'            shift, and go to state 5
'*'            shift, and go to state 6
'/'            shift, and go to state 7
```

In state 2, the automaton can only shift a symbol. For instance, because of the item 'exp -> exp . '+' exp', if the look-ahead is '+', it will be shifted on the parse stack, and the automaton control will jump to state 4, corresponding to the item 'exp -> exp '+' . exp'. Since there is no default action, any token other than those listed above will trigger a syntax error.

State 3 is named the *final state*, or the *accepting state*:

```
state 3


$accept  ->  exp $ .    (rule 0)


$default     accept
```

The initial rule is completed (the start-symbol and the end-of-input were read); the parser exits successfully.

The interpretation of states 4 to 7 is straightforward, and so is left to the reader.

```
state 4


exp  ->  exp '+' . exp    (rule 1)


NUM          shift, and go to state 1


exp          go to state 8


state 5
```

```
    exp  ->  exp '-' . exp    (rule 2)

    NUM          shift, and go to state 1

    exp          go to state 9

state 6

    exp  ->  exp '*' . exp    (rule 3)

    NUM          shift, and go to state 1

    exp          go to state 10

state 7

    exp  ->  exp '/' . exp    (rule 4)

    NUM          shift, and go to state 1

    exp          go to state 11
```

As was announced in the beginning of the report, 'State 8 conflicts: 1 shift/reduce':

```
state 8

    exp  ->  exp . '+' exp    (rule 1)
    exp  ->  exp '+' exp .    (rule 1)
    exp  ->  exp . '-' exp    (rule 2)
    exp  ->  exp . '*' exp    (rule 3)
    exp  ->  exp . '/' exp    (rule 4)

    '*'          shift, and go to state 6
    '/'          shift, and go to state 7

    '/'          [reduce using rule 1 (exp)]
    $default     reduce using rule 1 (exp)
```

Indeed, there are two actions associated to the look-ahead '/': either shifting (and going to state 7), or reducing rule 1. The conflict means that either the grammar is ambiguous, or the parser lacks information to make the right decision. Indeed the grammar is ambiguous. Since we did not specify the precedence of '/', the sentence 'NUM + NUM / NUM' can be parsed as 'NUM + (NUM / NUM)', which corresponds to shifting '/', or as '(NUM + NUM) / NUM', which corresponds to reducing rule 1.

Because in LALR(1) parsing a single decision can be made, Bison arbitrarily chose to disable the reduction. (See Section 5.2 [Shift/Reduce Conflicts], page 74.) Discarded actions are reported between square brackets.

Note that all the previous states had a single possible action: either shifting the next token and going to the corresponding state, or reducing a single rule. In the other cases, i.e., when shifting *and* reducing is possible or when *several* reductions are possible, the look-ahead is required to select the action. State 8 is one such state: if the look-ahead is '*' or '/' then the action is shifting, otherwise the action is reducing rule 1. In other words, the first two items, corresponding to rule 1, are not eligible when the look-ahead is '*', since we specified that '*' has higher precedence than '+'. More generally, some items are eligible only with some sets of possible look-aheads. When run with '--report=lookahead', Bison specifies these look-aheads:

```
state 8

    exp  ->  exp . '+' exp    [$, '+', '-', '/']    (rule 1)
    exp  ->  exp '+' exp .    [$, '+', '-', '/']    (rule 1)
    exp  ->  exp . '-' exp    (rule 2)
    exp  ->  exp . '*' exp    (rule 3)
    exp  ->  exp . '/' exp    (rule 4)


    '*'            shift, and go to state 6
    '/'            shift, and go to state 7


    '/'            [reduce using rule 1 (exp)]
    $default       reduce using rule 1 (exp)
```

The remaining states are similar:

```
state 9

    exp  ->  exp . '+' exp    (rule 1)
    exp  ->  exp . '-' exp    (rule 2)
    exp  ->  exp '-' exp .    (rule 2)
    exp  ->  exp . '*' exp    (rule 3)
    exp  ->  exp . '/' exp    (rule 4)


    '*'            shift, and go to state 6
    '/'            shift, and go to state 7


    '/'            [reduce using rule 2 (exp)]
    $default       reduce using rule 2 (exp)


state 10

    exp  ->  exp . '+' exp    (rule 1)
```

```
exp  ->  exp . '-' exp    (rule 2)
exp  ->  exp . '*' exp    (rule 3)
exp  ->  exp '*' exp .    (rule 3)
exp  ->  exp . '/' exp    (rule 4)


'/'          shift, and go to state 7


'/'          [reduce using rule 3 (exp)]
$default     reduce using rule 3 (exp)


state 11


exp  ->  exp . '+' exp    (rule 1)
exp  ->  exp . '-' exp    (rule 2)
exp  ->  exp . '*' exp    (rule 3)
exp  ->  exp . '/' exp    (rule 4)
exp  ->  exp '/' exp .    (rule 4)


'+'          shift, and go to state 4
'-'          shift, and go to state 5
'*'          shift, and go to state 6
'/'          shift, and go to state 7


'+'          [reduce using rule 4 (exp)]
'-'          [reduce using rule 4 (exp)]
'*'          [reduce using rule 4 (exp)]
'/'          [reduce using rule 4 (exp)]
$default     reduce using rule 4 (exp)
```

Observe that state 11 contains conflicts due to the lack of precedence of '/' with regard to '+', '-', and '*', but also because the associativity of '/' is not specified.

8.2 Tracing Your Parser

If a Bison grammar compiles properly but doesn't do what you want when it runs, the yydebug parser-trace feature can help you figure out why.

There are several means to enable compilation of trace facilities:

the macro YYDEBUG

>Define the macro YYDEBUG to a nonzero value when you compile the parser. This is compliant with POSIX Yacc. You could use '-DYYDEBUG=1' as a compiler option or you could put '#define YYDEBUG 1' in the prologue of the grammar file. (See Section 3.1.1 [The Prologue], page 43.)

the option '-t', '--debug'

>   Use the '-t' option when you run Bison. (See Chapter 9 [Invoking
>   Bison], page 101.) This is also POSIX compliant.

the directive '%debug'

>   Add the %debug directive. (See Section 3.7.9 [Bison Declaration
>   Summary], page 61.) This is a Bison extension, which will prove
>   useful when Bison outputs parsers for languages that don't use a pre-
>   processor. Unless POSIX and Yacc portability matter to you, this is the
>   preferred solution.

We suggest that you always enable the debug option so that debugging is always possible.

The trace facility outputs messages with macro calls of the form YYFPRINTF (stderr, *format*, *args*) where *format* and *args* are the usual printf format and arguments. If you define YYDEBUG to a nonzero value but do not define YYFPRINTF, <stdio.h> is automatically included and YYPRINTF is defined to fprintf.

Once you have compiled the program with trace facilities, the way to request a trace is to store a nonzero value in the variable yydebug. You can do this by making the C code do it (in main, perhaps), or you can alter the value with a C debugger.

Each step taken by the parser when yydebug is nonzero produces a line or two of trace information, written on stderr. The trace messages tell you these things:

- Each time the parser calls yylex, what kind of token was read.
- Each time a token is shifted, the depth and complete contents of the state stack (see Section 5.5 [Parser States], page 78).
- Each time a rule is reduced, which rule it is, and the complete contents of the state stack afterward.

To make sense of this information, it helps to refer to the listing file produced by the Bison '-v' option (see Chapter 9 [Invoking Bison], page 101). This file shows the meaning of each state in terms of positions in various rules, and also what each state will do with each possible input token. As you read the successive trace messages, you can see that the parser is functioning according to its specification in the listing file. Eventually you will arrive at the place where something undesirable happens, and you will see which parts of the grammar are to blame.

The parser file is a C program and you can use C debuggers on it, but it's not easy to interpret what it is doing. The parser function is a finite-state machine interpreter, and aside from the actions it executes the same code over and over. Only the values of variables show where in the grammar it is working.

The debugging information normally gives the token type of each token read, but not its semantic value. You can optionally define a macro named YYPRINT to provide a way to print the value. If you define YYPRINT, it should take three arguments. The parser will pass a standard I/O stream, the numeric code for the token type, and the token value (from yylval).

Here is an example of YYPRINT suitable for the multifunction calculator (see Section 2.5.1 [Declarations for mfcalc], page 36):

```
%{
  static void print_token_value (FILE *, int, YYSTYPE);
  #define YYPRINT(file, type, value) print_token_value (file, type, value)
%}

... %% ... %% ...

static void
print_token_value (FILE *file, int type, YYSTYPE value)
{
  if (type == VAR)
    fprintf (file, "%s", value.tptr->name);
  else if (type == NUM)
    fprintf (file, "%d", value.val);
}
```

9 Invoking Bison

The usual way to invoke Bison is as follows:

`bison` *infile*

Here *infile* is the grammar file name, which usually ends in '`.y`'. The parser file's name is made by replacing the '`.y`' with '`.tab.c`'. Thus, the '`bison foo.y`' file name yields '`foo.tab.c`', and the '`bison hack/foo.y`' file name yields '`hack/foo.tab.c`'. It's also possible, in case you are writing C++ code instead of C in your grammar file, to name it '`foo.ypp`' or '`foo.y++`'. Then, the output files will take an extension like the given one as input (respectively '`foo.tab.cpp`' and '`foo.tab.c++`'). This feature takes effect with all options that manipulate file names like '`-o`' or '`-d`'.

For example :

`bison -d` *infile.yxx*

will produce '`infile.tab.cxx`' and '`infile.tab.hxx`', and:

`bison -d -o` *output.c++* *infile.y*

will produce '`output.c++`' and '`outfile.h++`'.

For compatibility with POSIX, the standard Bison distribution also contains a shell script called `yacc` that invokes Bison with the '`-y`' option.

9.1 Bison Options

Bison supports both traditional single-letter options and mnemonic long option names. Long option names are indicated with '`--`' instead of '`-`'. Abbreviations for option names are allowed as long as they are unique. When a long option takes an argument, like '`--file-prefix`', connect the option name and the argument with '`=`'.

Here is a list of options that can be used with Bison, alphabetized by their single-letter option. It is followed by a cross key alphabetized by their long option.

Operations modes:

'`-h`'
'`--help`'   Print a summary of the command-line options to Bison and exit.

'`-V`'
'`--version`'
          Print the version number of Bison and exit.

'-y'

'--yacc'   Equivalent to '-o y.tab.c'; the parser output file is called
             'y.tab.c', and the other outputs are called 'y.output' and
             'y.tab.h'.   The purpose of this option is to imitate Yacc's
             output file name conventions.   Thus, the following shell script can
             substitute for Yacc. The Bison distribution contains such a script for
             compatibility with POSIX:

```
#! /bin/sh
bison -y "$"
```

Tuning the parser:

'-S file'

'--skeleton=file'

             Specify the skeleton to use. You probably don't need this option un-
             less you are developing Bison.

'-t'

'--debug'

             In the parser file, define the macro YYDEBUG to 1 if it is not already
             defined, so that the debugging facilities are compiled. (See Section 8.2
             [Tracing Your Parser], page 97.)

'--locations'

             Pretend that %locations was specified. (See Section 3.7.9 [Decl
             Summary], page 61.)

'-p prefix'

'--name-prefix=prefix'

             Pretend that %name-prefix="prefix" was specified.   (See Sec-
             tion 3.7.9 [Decl Summary], page 61.)

'-l'

'--no-lines'

             Don't put any #line preprocessor commands in the parser file. Or-
             dinarily Bison puts them in the parser file so that the C compiler and
             debuggers will associate errors with your source file, the grammar
             file. This option causes them to associate errors with the parser file,
             treating it as an independent source file in its own right.

'-n'

'--no-parser'

             Pretend that %no-parser was specified. (See Section 3.7.9 [Decl
             Summary], page 61.)

'-k'

'--token-table'

             Pretend that %token-table was specified. (See Section 3.7.9 [Decl
             Summary], page 61.)

Adjust the output:

'-d'
'--defines'

> Pretend that %defines was specified, i.e., write an extra output file containing macro definitions for the token type names defined in the grammar and the semantic value type YYSTYPE, as well as a few extern variable declarations. (See Section 3.7.9 [Decl Summary], page 61.)

'--defines=*defines-file*'

> Same as above, but save in the file *defines-file*.

'-b *file-prefix*'
'--file-prefix=*prefix*'

> Pretend that %verbose was specified, i.e, specify the prefix to use for all Bison output file names. (See Section 3.7.9 [Decl Summary], page 61.)

'-r *things*'
'--report=*things*'

> Write an extra output file containing verbose description of the comma-separated list of *things* among:

> state   Description of the grammar, conflicts (resolved and unresolved), and LALR automaton.

> lookahead
> > Implies state and augments the description of the automaton with each rule's look-ahead set.

> itemset   Implies state and augments the description of the automaton with the full set of items for each state, instead of only its core.

'-v'
'--verbose'

> Pretend that %verbose was specified, i.e, write an extra output file containing verbose descriptions of the grammar and parser. (See Section 3.7.9 [Decl Summary], page 61.)

'-o *filename*'
'--output=*filename*'

> Specify the *filename* for the parser file.

> The other output files' names are constructed from *filename* as described under the '-v' and '-d' options.

'-g'   Output a VCG definition of the LALR(1) grammar automaton computed by Bison. If the grammar file is 'foo.y', the VCG output file will be 'foo.vcg'.

'--graph=*graph-file*'
> The behavior of *–graph* is the same as '-g'. The only difference is that it has an optional argument that is the name of the output graph file name.

9.2 Option Cross Key

Here is an alphabetized list of long options to help you find the corresponding short option:

```
--debug . . . . . . . . . . . . . . . . . . . . . . -t
--defines . . . . . . . . . . . . . . . . . . . . . -d
--file-prefix . . . . . . . . . . . . . . . . . . . -b
--graph . . . . . . . . . . . . . . . . . . . . . . -g
--help . . . . . . . . . . . . . . . . . . . . . . . -h
--name-prefix . . . . . . . . . . . . . . . . . . . -p
--no-lines . . . . . . . . . . . . . . . . . . . . . -l
--no-parser . . . . . . . . . . . . . . . . . . . . -n
--output . . . . . . . . . . . . . . . . . . . . . . -o
--token-table . . . . . . . . . . . . . . . . . . . -k
--verbose . . . . . . . . . . . . . . . . . . . . . -v
--version . . . . . . . . . . . . . . . . . . . . . -V
--yacc . . . . . . . . . . . . . . . . . . . . . . . -y
```

9.3 Yacc Library

The Yacc library contains default implementations of the yyerror and main functions. These default implementations are normally not useful, but POSIX requires them. To use the Yacc library, link your program with the '-ly' option. Note that Bison's implementation of the Yacc library is distributed under the terms of the GNU General Public License. (See [Copying], page 5.)

If you use the Yacc library's yyerror function, you should declare yyerror as follows:

```
int yyerror (char const *);
```

Bison ignores the int value returned by this yyerror. If you use the Yacc library's main function, your yyparse function should have the following type signature:

```
int yyparse (void);
```

10 Frequently Asked Questions

Here are some of the questions that occasionally come up about Bison.

10.1 Parser Stack Overflow

My parser returns an error with a 'parser stack overflow'
message. What can I do?

This question is already addressed elsewhere, in Section 3.4 [Recursive Rules],
page 48.

10.2 How Can I Reset the Parser

The following phenomenon has several symptoms, resulting in the following
typical questions:

I invoke yyparse several times, and on correct input it works
properly; but when a parse error is found, all the other calls fail
too. How can I reset the error flag of yyparse?

or

My parser includes support for an '#include'-like feature, in
which case I run yyparse from yyparse. This fails
although I did specify I needed a %pure-parser.

These problems typically come not from Bison itself, but from Lex-generated
scanners. Because these scanners use large buffers for speed, they might not notice
a change of input file. As a demonstration, consider the following source file,
'first-line.l':

```
%{
#include <stdio.h>
#include <stdlib.h>
%}
%%
.*\n    ECHO; return 1;
%%
int
yyparse (char const *file)
{
  yyin = fopen (file, "r");
  if (!yyin)
    exit (2);
  /* One token only. */
  yylex ();
  if (fclose (yyin) != 0)
    exit (3);
```

```
    return 0;
  }

  int
  main (void)
  {
    yyparse ("input");
    yyparse ("input");
    return 0;
  }
```

If the file 'input' contains

```
input:1: Hello,
input:2: World!
```

then instead of getting the first line twice, you get:

```
$ flex -ofirst-line.c first-line.l
$ gcc  -ofirst-line    first-line.c -ll
$ ./first-line
input:1: Hello,
input:2: World!
```

Therefore, whenever you change yyin, you must tell the Lex-generated scanner to discard its current buffer and switch to the new one. This depends upon your implementation of Lex; see its documentation for more. For Flex, it suffices to call 'YY_FLUSH_BUFFER' after each change to yyin. If your Flex-generated scanner needs to read from several input streams to handle features like include files, you might consider using Flex functions like 'yy_switch_to_buffer' that manipulate multiple input buffers.

10.3 Strings are Destroyed

My parser seems to destroy old strings, or maybe it loses track of them. Instead of reporting '"foo", "bar"', it reports '"bar", "bar"', or even '"foo\nbar", "bar"'.

This error is probably the single most frequent "bug report" sent to Bison lists, but is only concerned with a misunderstanding of the role of scanner. Consider the following Lex code:

```
%{
#include <stdio.h>
char *yylval = NULL;
%}
%%
.*    yylval = yytext; return 1;
\n    /* IGNORE */
%%
```

```
int
main ()
{
  /* Similar to using $1, $2 in a Bison action. */
  char *fst = (yylex (), yylval);
  char *snd = (yylex (), yylval);
  printf ("\"%s\", \"%s\"\n", fst, snd);
  return 0;
}
```

If you compile and run this code, you get:

```
$ flex -osplit-lines.c split-lines.l
$ gcc  -osplit-lines  split-lines.c -ll
$ printf 'one\ntwo\n' | ./split-lines
"one
two", "two"
```

this is because `yytext` is a buffer provided for *reading* in the action, but if you want to keep it, you have to duplicate it (e.g., using `strdup`). Note that the output may depend on how your implementation of Lex handles `yytext`. For instance, when given the Lex compatibility option '-l' (which triggers the option '%array') Flex generates a different behavior:

```
$ flex -l -osplit-lines.c split-lines.l
$ gcc    -osplit-lines   split-lines.c -ll
$ printf 'one\ntwo\n' | ./split-lines
"two", "two"
```

10.4 C++ Parsers

How can I generate parsers in C++?

We are working on a C++ output for Bison, but unfortunately, for lack of time, the skeleton is not finished. It is functional, but in numerous respects, it will require additional work which *might* break backward compatibility. Since the skeleton for C++ is not documented, we do not consider ourselves bound to this interface, nevertheless, as much as possible we will try to keep compatibility.

Another possibility is to use the regular C parsers, and to compile them with a C++ compiler. This works properly, provided that you bear some simple C++ rules in mind, such as not including "real classes" (i.e., structure with constructors) in unions. Therefore, in the `%union`, use pointers to classes, or better yet, a single pointer type to the root of your lexical/syntactic hierarchy.

10.5 Implementing Loops

My simple calculator supports variables, assignments, and functions, but how can I implement loops?

Although very pedagogical, the examples included in the document blur the distinction to make between the parser—whose job is to recover the structure of a text and to transmit it to subsequent modules of the program—and the processing (such as the execution) of this structure. This works well with so called straight line programs, i.e., precisely those that have a straightforward execution model: execute simple instructions one after the others.

If you want a richer model, you will probably need to use the parser to construct a tree that does represent the structure it has recovered; this tree is usually called the *abstract syntax tree*, or AST for short. Then, walking through this tree, traversing it in various ways, will enable treatments such as its execution or its translation, which will result in an interpreter or a compiler.

This topic is way beyond the scope of this manual, and the reader is invited to consult the dedicated literature.

Appendix A Bison Symbols

@$ Variable
  In an action, the location of the left hand side of the rule. (See Section 3.6
  [Locations Overview], page 53.)

@*n*   Variable
  In an action, the location of the *n*-th symbol of the right hand side of the rule.
  (See Section 3.6 [Locations Overview], page 53.)

$$ Variable
  In an action, the semantic value of the left hand side of the rule. (See Sec-
  tion 3.5.3 [Actions], page 49.)

$*n*   Variable
  In an action, the semantic value of the *n*-th symbol of the right hand side of the
  rule. (See Section 3.5.3 [Actions], page 49.)

$accept   Symbol
  The predefined nonterminal whose only rule is '`$accept` : *start* `$end`', where
  start is the start-symbol. (See Section 3.7.7 [The Start-Symbol], page 60.) It
  cannot be used in the grammar.

$end   Symbol
  The predefined token marking the end of the token stream. It cannot be used in
  the grammar.

$undefined   Symbol
  The predefined token onto which all undefined values returned by `yylex` are
  mapped. It cannot be used in the grammar. Use `error` instead.

error   Symbol
  A token name reserved for error recovery. This token may be used in grammar
  rules so as to allow the Bison parser to recognize an error in the grammar without
  halting the process. In effect, a sentence containing an error may be recognized
  as valid. On a syntax error, the token `error` becomes the current look-ahead
  token. Actions corresponding to `error` are then executed, and the look-ahead
  token is reset to the token that originally caused the violation. (See Chapter 6
  [Error Recovery], page 85.)

YYABORT   Macro
  Macro to pretend that an unrecoverable syntax error has occurred, by making
  `yyparse` return 1 immediately. The error-reporting function `yyerror` is not
  called. (See Section 4.1 [The Parser Function `yyparse`], page 65.)

YYACCEPT   Macro

Macro to pretend that a complete utterance of the language has been read, by making `yyparse` return 0 immediately. (See Section 4.1 [The Parser Function `yyparse`], page 65.)

YYBACKUP   Macro

Macro to discard a value from the parser stack and fake a look-ahead token. (See Section 4.4 [Special Features for Use in Actions], page 71.)

YYDEBUG   Macro

Macro to define to equip the parser with tracing code. (See Section 8.2 [Tracing Your Parser], page 97.)

YYERROR   Macro

Macro to pretend that a syntax error has just been detected: call `yyerror` and then perform normal error recovery if possible, or if recovery is impossible make `yyparse` return 1. (See Chapter 6 [Error Recovery], page 85.)

YYERROR_VERBOSE   Macro

An obsolete macro that you define with `#define` in the prologue to request verbose, specific error message strings when `yyerror` is called. It doesn't matter what definition you use for YYERROR_VERBOSE, only whether you define it. Using `%error-verbose` is preferred.

YYINITDEPTH   Macro

Macro for specifying the initial size of the parser stack. (See Section 5.9 [Stack Overflow], page 84.)

YYLEX_PARAM   Macro

An obsolete macro for specifying an extra argument (or list of extra arguments) for `yyparse` to pass to `yylex`. The use of this macro is deprecated, and is supported only for Yacc-like parsers. (See Section 4.2.4 [Calling Conventions for Pure Parsers], page 68.)

YYLTYPE   Type

Data type of `yylloc`; by default, a structure with four members. (See Section 3.6.1 [Data Types of Locations], page 53.)

YYMAXDEPTH   Macro

Macro for specifying the maximum size of the parser stack. (See Section 5.9 [Stack Overflow], page 84.)

YYPARSE_PARAM   Macro

An obsolete macro for specifying the name of a parameter that `yyparse` should accept. The use of this macro is deprecated, and is supported only for Yacc-like parsers. (See Section 4.2.4 [Calling Conventions for Pure Parsers], page 68.)

YYRECOVERING   Macro
Macro whose value indicates whether the parser is recovering from a syntax error. (See Section 4.4 [Special Features for Use in Actions], page 71.)

YYSTACK_USE_ALLOCA   Macro
Macro used to control the use of `alloca`. If defined to '0', the parser will not use `alloca` but `malloc` when trying to grow its internal stacks. Do *not* define `YYSTACK_USE_ALLOCA` to anything else.

YYSTYPE   Type
Data type of semantic values; `int` by default. (See Section 3.5.1 [Data Types of Semantic Values], page 49.)

yychar   Variable
External integer variable that contains the integer value of the current look-ahead token. In a pure parser, it is a local variable within `yyparse`. Error recovery rule actions may examine this variable. (See Section 4.4 [Special Features for Use in Actions], page 71.)

yyclearin   Variable
Macro used in error recovery rule actions. It clears the previous look-ahead token. (See Chapter 6 [Error Recovery], page 85.)

yydebug   Variable
External integer variable set to zero by default. If `yydebug` is given a nonzero value, the parser will output information on input symbols and parser action. (See Section 8.2 [Tracing Your Parser], page 97.)

yyerrok   Macro
Macro to cause parser to recover immediately to its normal mode after a syntax error. (See Chapter 6 [Error Recovery], page 85.)

yyerror   Function
User-supplied function to be called by `yyparse` on error. (See Section 4.3 [The Error Reporting Function `yyerror`], page 69.)

yylex   Function
User-supplied lexical analyzer function, called with no arguments to get the next token. (See Section 4.2 [The Lexical Analyzer Function `yylex`], page 66.)

yylval   Variable
External variable in which `yylex` should place the semantic value associated with a token. In a pure parser, it is a local variable within `yyparse`, and its address is passed to `yylex`. (See Section 4.2.2 [Semantic Values of Tokens], page 67.)

yylloc   Variable
> External variable in which `yylex` should place the line and column numbers
> associated with a token. In a pure parser, it is a local variable within `yyparse`,
> and its address is passed to `yylex`. You can ignore this variable if you don't use
> the '@' feature in the grammar actions. (See Section 4.2.3 [Textual Locations of
> Tokens], page 68.)

yynerrs   Variable
> Global variable that Bison increments each time there is a syntax error. In a
> pure parser, it is a local variable within `yyparse`. See Section 4.3 [The Error
> Reporting Function `yyerror`], page 69.

yyparse   Function
> The parser function produced by Bison; call this function to start parsing. (See
> Section 4.1 [The Parser Function `yyparse`], page 65.)

%debug   Directive
> Equip the parser for debugging. (See Section 3.7.9 [Decl Summary], page 61.)

%defines   Directive
> Bison declaration to create a header file meant for the scanner. (See Sec-
> tion 3.7.9 [Decl Summary], page 61.)

%destructor   Directive
> Specify how the parser should reclaim the memory associated to discarded sym-
> bols. (See Section 3.7.5 [Freeing Discarded Symbols], page 58.)

%dprec   Directive
> Bison declaration to assign a precedence to a rule that is used at parse time to re-
> solve reduce/reduce conflicts. (See Section 1.5 [Writing GLR Parsers], page 16.)

%error-verbose   Directive
> Bison declaration to request verbose, specific error message strings when
> `yyerror` is called.

%file-prefix="*prefix*"   Directive
> Bison declaration to set the prefix of the output files. (See Section 3.7.9 [Decl
> Summary], page 61.)

%glr-parser   Directive
> Bison declaration to produce a GLR parser. (See Section 1.5 [Writing GLR
> Parsers], page 16.)

%left   Directive
> Bison declaration to assign left associativity to token(s). (See Section 3.7.2
> [Operator Precedence], page 57.)

%lex-param { *argument-declaration* }   Directive
> Bison declaration to specifying an additional parameter that `yylex` should accept. (See Section 4.2.4 [Calling Conventions for Pure Parsers], page 68.)

%merge   Directive
> Bison declaration to assign a merging function to a rule. If there is a reduce/reduce conflict with a rule having the same merging function, the function is applied to the two semantic values to get a single result. (See Section 1.5 [Writing GLR Parsers], page 16.)

%name-prefix="*prefix*"   Directive
> Bison declaration to rename the external symbols. (See Section 3.7.9 [Decl Summary], page 61.)

%no-lines   Directive
> Bison declaration to avoid generating `#line` directives in the parser file. (See Section 3.7.9 [Decl Summary], page 61.)

%nonassoc   Directive
> Bison declaration to assign nonassociativity to token(s). (See Section 3.7.2 [Operator Precedence], page 57.)

%output="*filename*"   Directive
> Bison declaration to set the name of the parser file. (See Section 3.7.9 [Decl Summary], page 61.)

%parse-param { *argument-declaration* }   Directive
> Bison declaration to specifying an additional parameter that `yyparse` should accept. (See Section 4.1 [The Parser Function `yyparse`], page 65.)

%prec   Directive
> Bison declaration to assign a precedence to a specific rule. (See Section 5.4 [Context-Dependent Precedence], page 77.)

%pure-parser   Directive
> Bison declaration to request a pure (reentrant) parser. (See Section 3.7.8 [A Pure (Reentrant) Parser], page 60.)

%right   Directive
> Bison declaration to assign right associativity to token(s). (See Section 3.7.2 [Operator Precedence], page 57.)

%start   Directive
> Bison declaration to specify the start-symbol. (See Section 3.7.7 [The Start-Symbol], page 60.)

%token   Directive
> Bison declaration to declare token(s) without specifying precedence. (See Section 3.7.1 [Token Type Names], page 56.)

%token-table   Directive
> Bison declaration to include a token name table in the parser file. (See Section 3.7.9 [Decl Summary], page 61.)

%type   Directive
> Bison declaration to declare nonterminals. (See Section 3.7.4 [Nonterminal Symbols], page 58.)

%union   Directive
> Bison declaration to specify several possible data types for semantic values. (See Section 3.7.3 [The Collection of Value Types], page 58.)

These are the punctuation and delimiters used in Bison input:

%%   Delimiter
> Delimiter used to separate the grammar rule section from the Bison declarations section or the epilogue. (See Section 1.9 [The Overall Layout of a Bison Grammar], page 21.)

%{ *code* %}   Delimiter
> All code listed between '%{' and '%}' is copied directly to the output file uninterpreted. Such code forms the prologue of the input file. (See Section 3.1 [Outline of a Bison Grammar], page 43.)

/*...*/   Construct
> Comment delimiters, as in C.

:   Delimiter
> Separates a rule's result from its components. (See Section 3.3 [Syntax of Grammar Rules], page 47.)

;   Delimiter
> Terminates a rule. (See Section 3.3 [Syntax of Grammar Rules], page 47.)

| Delimiter
> Separates alternate rules for the same result nonterminal. (See Section 3.3 [Syntax of Grammar Rules], page 47.)

Appendix B Glossary

Backus-Naur Form (BNF; also called "Backus Normal Form")
> Formal method of specifying context-free grammars originally pro-
> posed by John Backus, and slightly improved by Peter Naur in his
> 1960-01-02 committee document contributing to what became the Al-
> gol 60 report. (See Section 1.1 [Languages and Context-Free Gram-
> mars], page 13.)

Context-free grammars
> Grammars specified as rules that can be applied regardless of context.
> Thus, if there is a rule that says that an integer can be used as an
> expression, integers are allowed *anywhere* an expression is permitted.
> (See Section 1.1 [Languages and Context-Free Grammars], page 13.)

Dynamic allocation
> Allocation of memory that occurs during execution, rather than at
> compile time or on entry to a function.

Empty string
> Analogous to the empty set in set theory, the empty string is a charac-
> ter string of length zero.

Finite-state stack machine
> A "machine" that has discrete states in which it is said to exist at each
> instant in time. As input to the machine is processed, the machine
> moves from state to state as specified by the logic of the machine.
> In the case of the parser, the input is the language being parsed, and
> the states correspond to various stages in the grammar rules. (See
> Chapter 5 [The Bison Parser Algorithm], page 73.)

Generalized LR (GLR)
> A parsing algorithm that can handle all context-free grammars, in-
> cluding those that are not LALR(1). It resolves situations that Bison's
> usual LALR(1) algorithm cannot by effectively splitting off multiple
> parsers, trying all possible parsers, and discarding those that fail in
> the light of additional right context. (See Section 5.8 [Generalized LR
> Parsing], page 82.)

Grouping   A language construct that is (in general) grammatically divisible; for
> example, 'expression' or 'declaration' in C. (See Section 1.1 [Lan-
> guages and Context-Free Grammars], page 13.)

Infix operator
> An arithmetic operator that is placed between the operands on which
> it performs some operation.

Input stream
> A continuous flow of data between devices or programs.

Language construct

> One of the typical usage schemas of the language. For example, one of the constructs of the C language is the `if` statement. (See Section 1.1 [Languages and Context-Free Grammars], page 13.)

Left associativity

> Operators having left associativity are analyzed from left to right: 'a+b+c' first computes 'a+b' and then combines with 'c'. (See Section 5.3 [Operator Precedence], page 75.)

Left recursion

> A rule whose result symbol is also its first component symbol; for example, 'expseq1 : expseq1 ',' exp;'. (See Section 3.4 [Recursive Rules], page 48.)

Left-to-right parsing

> Parsing a sentence of a language by analyzing it token by token from left to right. (See Chapter 5 [The Bison Parser Algorithm], page 73.)

Lexical analyzer (scanner)

> A function that reads an input stream and returns tokens one by one. (See Section 4.2 [The Lexical Analyzer Function `yylex`], page 66.)

Lexical tie-in

> A flag set by actions in the grammar rules that alters the way tokens are parsed. (See Section 7.2 [Lexical Tie-Ins], page 88.)

Literal string token

> A token that consists of two or more fixed characters. (See Section 3.2 [Symbols], page 44.)

Look-ahead token

> A token already read but not yet shifted. (See Section 5.1 [Look-Ahead Tokens], page 73.)

LALR(1)   The class of context-free grammars that Bison (like most other parser generators) can handle; a subset of LR(1). (See Section 5.7 [Mysterious Reduce/Reduce Conflicts], page 80.)

LR(1)   The class of context-free grammars in which at most one token of look-ahead is needed to disambiguate the parsing of any piece of input.

Nonterminal symbol

> A grammar symbol standing for a grammatical construct that can be expressed through rules in terms of smaller constructs; in other words, a construct that is not a token. (See Section 3.2 [Symbols], page 44.)

Parser   A function that recognizes valid sentences of a language by analyzing the syntax structure of a set of tokens passed to it from a lexical analyzer.

Postfix operator

    An arithmetic operator that is placed after the operands upon which it performs some operation.

Reduction   Replacing a string of nonterminals and/or terminals with a single nonterminal, according to a grammar rule. (See Chapter 5 [The Bison Parser Algorithm], page 73.)

Reentrant   A reentrant subprogram is a subprogram that can be in invoked any number of times in parallel, without interference between the various invocations. (See Section 3.7.8 [A Pure (Reentrant) Parser], page 60.)

Reverse polish notation

    A language in which all operators are postfix operators.

Right recursion

    A rule whose result symbol is also its last component symbol; for example, 'expseq1: exp ',' expseq1;'. (See Section 3.4 [Recursive Rules], page 48.)

Semantics   In computer languages, the semantics is specified by the actions taken for each instance of the language, i.e., the meaning of each statement. (See Section 3.5 [Defining Language Semantics], page 48.)

Shift   A parser is said to shift when it makes the choice of analyzing further input from the stream rather than reducing immediately some already recognized rule. (See Chapter 5 [The Bison Parser Algorithm], page 73.)

Single-character literal

    A single character that is recognized and interpreted as is. (See Section 1.2 [From Formal Rules to Bison Input], page 15.)

Start-symbol

    The nonterminal symbol that stands for a complete valid utterance in the language being parsed. The start-symbol is usually listed as the first nonterminal symbol in a language specification. (See Section 3.7.7 [The Start-Symbol], page 60.)

Symbol table

    A data structure where symbol names and associated data are stored during parsing to allow for recognition and use of existing information in repeated uses of a symbol. (See Section 2.5 [Multifunction Calc], page 35.)

Syntax error

    An error encountered during parsing of an input stream due to invalid syntax. (See Chapter 6 [Error Recovery], page 85.)

Token   A basic, grammatically indivisible unit of a language. The symbol that describes a token in the grammar is a terminal symbol. The input of the Bison parser is a stream of tokens which comes from the lexical analyzer. (See Section 3.2 [Symbols], page 44.)

Terminal symbol

A grammar symbol that has no rules in the grammar and therefore is grammatically indivisible. The piece of text it represents is a token. (See Section 1.1 [Languages and Context-Free Grammars], page 13.)

Appendix C Copying This Manual

C.1 GNU Free Documentation License

Version 1.2, November 2002

Copyright © 2000,2001,2002 Free Software Foundation, Inc.
59 Temple Place, Suite 330, Boston, MA 02111-1307, USA

Everyone is permitted to copy and distribute verbatim copies
of this license document, but changing it is not allowed.

0. PREAMBLE

The purpose of this License is to make a manual, textbook, or other functional
and useful document *free* in the sense of freedom: to assure everyone the
effective freedom to copy and redistribute it, with or without modifying it,
either commercially or noncommercially. Secondarily, this License preserves
for the author and publisher a way to get credit for their work, while not being
considered responsible for modifications made by others.

This License is a kind of "copyleft", which means that derivative works of
the document must themselves be free in the same sense. It complements the
GNU General Public License, which is a copyleft license designed for free
software.

We have designed this License in order to use it for manuals for free software,
because free software needs free documentation: a free program should come
with manuals providing the same freedoms that the software does. But this
License is not limited to software manuals; it can be used for any textual work,
regardless of subject matter or whether it is published as a printed book. We
recommend this License principally for works whose purpose is instruction or
reference.

1. APPLICABILITY AND DEFINITIONS

This License applies to any manual or other work, in any medium, that contains a notice placed by the copyright holder saying it can be distributed under
the terms of this License. Such a notice grants a world-wide, royalty-free
license, unlimited in duration, to use that work under the conditions stated
herein. The "Document", below, refers to any such manual or work. Any
member of the public is a licensee, and is addressed as "you". You accept the
license if you copy, modify or distribute the work in a way requiring permission under copyright law.

A "Modified Version" of the Document means any work containing the Document or a portion of it, either copied verbatim, or with modifications and/or
translated into another language.

A "Secondary Section" is a named appendix or a front-matter section of the
Document that deals exclusively with the relationship of the publishers or authors of the Document to the Document's overall subject (or to related matters)

and contains nothing that could fall directly within that overall subject. (Thus, if the Document is in part a textbook of mathematics, a Secondary Section may not explain any mathematics.) The relationship could be a matter of historical connection with the subject or with related matters, or of legal, commercial, philosophical, ethical or political position regarding them.

The "Invariant Sections" are certain Secondary Sections whose titles are designated, as being those of Invariant Sections, in the notice that says that the Document is released under this License. If a section does not fit the above definition of Secondary then it is not allowed to be designated as Invariant. The Document may contain zero Invariant Sections. If the Document does not identify any Invariant Sections then there are none.

The "Cover Texts" are certain short passages of text that are listed, as Front-Cover Texts or Back-Cover Texts, in the notice that says that the Document is released under this License. A Front-Cover Text may be at most 5 words, and a Back-Cover Text may be at most 25 words.

A "Transparent" copy of the Document means a machine-readable copy, represented in a format whose specification is available to the general public, that is suitable for revising the document straightforwardly with generic text editors or (for images composed of pixels) generic paint programs or (for drawings) some widely available drawing editor, and that is suitable for input to text formatters or for automatic translation to a variety of formats suitable for input to text formatters. A copy made in an otherwise Transparent file format whose markup, or absence of markup, has been arranged to thwart or discourage subsequent modification by readers is not Transparent. An image format is not Transparent if used for any substantial amount of text. A copy that is not "Transparent" is called "Opaque".

Examples of suitable formats for Transparent copies include plain ASCII without markup, Texinfo input format, LaTeX input format, SGML or XML using a publicly available DTD, and standard-conforming simple HTML, PostScript or PDF designed for human modification. Examples of transparent image formats include PNG, XCF and JPG. Opaque formats include proprietary formats that can be read and edited only by proprietary word processors, SGML or XML for which the DTD and/or processing tools are not generally available, and the machine-generated HTML, PostScript or PDF produced by some word processors for output purposes only.

The "Title Page" means, for a printed book, the title page itself, plus such following pages as are needed to hold, legibly, the material this License requires to appear in the title page. For works in formats which do not have any title page as such, "Title Page" means the text near the most prominent appearance of the work's title, preceding the beginning of the body of the text.

A section "Entitled XYZ" means a named subunit of the Document whose title either is precisely XYZ or contains XYZ in parentheses following text that translates XYZ in another language. (Here XYZ stands for a specific section name mentioned below, such as "Acknowledgements", "Dedications", "Endorsements", or "History".) To "Preserve the Title" of such a section when you modify the Document means that it remains a section "Entitled XYZ" according to this definition.

The Document may include Warranty Disclaimers next to the notice which states that this License applies to the Document. These Warranty Disclaimers are considered to be included by reference in this License, but only as regards disclaiming warranties: any other implication that these Warranty Disclaimers may have is void and has no effect on the meaning of this License.

2. VERBATIM COPYING

You may copy and distribute the Document in any medium, either commercially or noncommercially, provided that this License, the copyright notices, and the license notice saying this License applies to the Document are reproduced in all copies, and that you add no other conditions whatsoever to those of this License. You may not use technical measures to obstruct or control the reading or further copying of the copies you make or distribute. However, you may accept compensation in exchange for copies. If you distribute a large enough number of copies you must also follow the conditions in section 3.

You may also lend copies, under the same conditions stated above, and you may publicly display copies.

3. COPYING IN QUANTITY

If you publish printed copies (or copies in media that commonly have printed covers) of the Document, numbering more than 100, and the Document's license notice requires Cover Texts, you must enclose the copies in covers that carry, clearly and legibly, all these Cover Texts: Front-Cover Texts on the front cover, and Back-Cover Texts on the back cover. Both covers must also clearly and legibly identify you as the publisher of these copies. The front cover must present the full title with all words of the title equally prominent and visible. You may add other material on the covers in addition. Copying with changes limited to the covers, as long as they preserve the title of the Document and satisfy these conditions, can be treated as verbatim copying in other respects.

If the required texts for either cover are too voluminous to fit legibly, you should put the first ones listed (as many as fit reasonably) on the actual cover, and continue the rest onto adjacent pages.

If you publish or distribute Opaque copies of the Document numbering more than 100, you must either include a machine-readable Transparent copy along with each Opaque copy, or state in or with each Opaque copy a computer-network location from which the general network-using public has access to download using public-standard network protocols a complete Transparent copy of the Document, free of added material. If you use the latter option, you must take reasonably prudent steps, when you begin distribution of Opaque copies in quantity, to ensure that this Transparent copy will remain thus accessible at the stated location until at least one year after the last time you distribute an Opaque copy (directly or through your agents or retailers) of that edition to the public.

It is requested, but not required, that you contact the authors of the Document well before redistributing any large number of copies, to give them a chance to provide you with an updated version of the Document.

4. MODIFICATIONS

You may copy and distribute a Modified Version of the Document under the conditions of sections 2 and 3 above, provided that you release the Modified Version under precisely this License, with the Modified Version filling the role of the Document, thus licensing distribution and modification of the Modified Version to whoever possesses a copy of it. In addition, you must do these things in the Modified Version:

A. Use in the Title Page (and on the covers, if any) a title distinct from that of the Document, and from those of previous versions (which should, if there were any, be listed in the History section of the Document). You may use the same title as a previous version if the original publisher of that version gives permission.

B. List on the Title Page, as authors, one or more persons or entities responsible for authorship of the modifications in the Modified Version, together with at least five of the principal authors of the Document (all of its principal authors, if it has fewer than five), unless they release you from this requirement.

C. State on the Title page the name of the publisher of the Modified Version, as the publisher.

D. Preserve all the copyright notices of the Document.

E. Add an appropriate copyright notice for your modifications adjacent to the other copyright notices.

F. Include, immediately after the copyright notices, a license notice giving the public permission to use the Modified Version under the terms of this License, in the form shown in the Addendum below.

G. Preserve in that license notice the full lists of Invariant Sections and required Cover Texts given in the Document's license notice.

H. Include an unaltered copy of this License.

I. Preserve the section Entitled "History", Preserve its Title, and add to it an item stating at least the title, year, new authors, and publisher of the Modified Version as given on the Title Page. If there is no section Entitled "History" in the Document, create one stating the title, year, authors, and publisher of the Document as given on its Title Page, then add an item describing the Modified Version as stated in the previous sentence.

J. Preserve the network location, if any, given in the Document for public access to a Transparent copy of the Document, and likewise the network locations given in the Document for previous versions it was based on. These may be placed in the "History" section. You may omit a network location for a work that was published at least four years before the Document itself, or if the original publisher of the version it refers to gives permission.

K. For any section Entitled "Acknowledgements" or "Dedications", Preserve the Title of the section, and preserve in the section all the substance and tone of each of the contributor acknowledgements and/or dedications given therein.

L. Preserve all the Invariant Sections of the Document, unaltered in their text and in their titles. Section numbers or the equivalent are not considered part of the section titles.

M. Delete any section Entitled "Endorsements". Such a section may not be included in the Modified Version.

N. Do not retitle any existing section to be Entitled "Endorsements" or to conflict in title with any Invariant Section.

O. Preserve any Warranty Disclaimers.

If the Modified Version includes new front-matter sections or appendices that qualify as Secondary Sections and contain no material copied from the Document, you may at your option designate some or all of these sections as invariant. To do this, add their titles to the list of Invariant Sections in the Modified Version's license notice. These titles must be distinct from any other section titles.

You may add a section Entitled "Endorsements", provided it contains nothing but endorsements of your Modified Version by various parties—for example, statements of peer review or that the text has been approved by an organization as the authoritative definition of a standard.

You may add a passage of up to five words as a Front-Cover Text, and a passage of up to 25 words as a Back-Cover Text, to the end of the list of Cover Texts in the Modified Version. Only one passage of Front-Cover Text and one of Back-Cover Text may be added by (or through arrangements made by) any one entity. If the Document already includes a cover text for the same cover, previously added by you or by arrangement made by the same entity you are acting on behalf of, you may not add another; but you may replace the old one, on explicit permission from the previous publisher that added the old one.

The author(s) and publisher(s) of the Document do not by this License give permission to use their names for publicity for or to assert or imply endorsement of any Modified Version.

5. COMBINING DOCUMENTS

You may combine the Document with other documents released under this License, under the terms defined in section 4 above for modified versions, provided that you include in the combination all of the Invariant Sections of all of the original documents, unmodified, and list them all as Invariant Sections of your combined work in its license notice, and that you preserve all their Warranty Disclaimers.

The combined work need only contain one copy of this License, and multiple identical Invariant Sections may be replaced with a single copy. If there are multiple Invariant Sections with the same name but different contents, make the title of each such section unique by adding at the end of it, in parentheses, the name of the original author or publisher of that section if known, or else a unique number. Make the same adjustment to the section titles in the list of Invariant Sections in the license notice of the combined work.

In the combination, you must combine any sections Entitled "History" in the various original documents, forming one section Entitled "History"; likewise combine any sections Entitled "Acknowledgements", and any sections Entitled "Dedications". You must delete all sections Entitled "Endorsements."

6. COLLECTIONS OF DOCUMENTS

You may make a collection consisting of the Document and other documents released under this License, and replace the individual copies of this License in the various documents with a single copy that is included in the collection, provided that you follow the rules of this License for verbatim copying of each of the documents in all other respects.

You may extract a single document from such a collection, and distribute it individually under this License, provided you insert a copy of this License into the extracted document, and follow this License in all other respects regarding verbatim copying of that document.

7. AGGREGATION WITH INDEPENDENT WORKS

A compilation of the Document or its derivatives with other separate and independent documents or works, in or on a volume of a storage or distribution medium, is called an "aggregate" if the copyright resulting from the compilation is not used to limit the legal rights of the compilation's users beyond what the individual works permit. When the Document is included in an aggregate, this License does not apply to the other works in the aggregate which are not themselves derivative works of the Document.

If the Cover Text requirement of section 3 is applicable to these copies of the Document, then if the Document is less than one half of the entire aggregate, the Document's Cover Texts may be placed on covers that bracket the Document within the aggregate, or the electronic equivalent of covers if the Document is in electronic form. Otherwise they must appear on printed covers that bracket the whole aggregate.

8. TRANSLATION

Translation is considered a kind of modification, so you may distribute translations of the Document under the terms of section 4. Replacing Invariant Sections with translations requires special permission from their copyright holders, but you may include translations of some or all Invariant Sections in addition to the original versions of these Invariant Sections. You may include a translation of this License, and all the license notices in the Document, and any Warranty Disclaimers, provided that you also include the original English version of this License and the original versions of those notices and disclaimers. In case of a disagreement between the translation and the original version of this License or a notice or disclaimer, the original version will prevail.

If a section in the Document is Entitled "Acknowledgements", "Dedications", or "History", the requirement (section 4) to Preserve its Title (section 1) will typically require changing the actual title.

9. TERMINATION

You may not copy, modify, sublicense, or distribute the Document except as expressly provided for under this License. Any other attempt to copy, modify, sublicense or distribute the Document is void, and will automatically terminate your rights under this License. However, parties who have received copies, or rights, from you under this License will not have their licenses terminated so long as such parties remain in full compliance.

10. FUTURE REVISIONS OF THIS LICENSE

The Free Software Foundation may publish new, revised versions of the GNU Free Documentation License from time to time. Such new versions will be similar in spirit to the present version, but may differ in detail to address new problems or concerns. See `http://www.gnu.org/copyleft/`.

Each version of the License is given a distinguishing version number. If the Document specifies that a particular numbered version of this License "or any later version" applies to it, you have the option of following the terms and conditions either of that specified version or of any later version that has been published (not as a draft) by the Free Software Foundation. If the Document does not specify a version number of this License, you may choose any version ever published (not as a draft) by the Free Software Foundation.

C.1.1 ADDENDUM: How to use this License for your documents

To use this License in a document you have written, include a copy of the License in the document and put the following copyright and license notices just after the title page:

```
Copyright (C)  year   your name.
Permission is granted to copy, distribute and/or modify this document
under the terms of the GNU Free Documentation License, Version 1.2
or any later version published by the Free Software Foundation;
with no Invariant Sections, no Front-Cover Texts, and no Back-Cover Texts.
A copy of the license is included in the section entitled ''GNU
Free Documentation License''.
```

If you have Invariant Sections, Front-Cover Texts and Back-Cover Texts, replace the "with...Texts." line with this:

```
with the Invariant Sections being list their titles, with
the Front-Cover Texts being list, and with the Back-Cover Texts
being list.
```

If you have Invariant Sections without Cover Texts, or some other combination of the three, merge those two alternatives to suit the situation.

If your document contains nontrivial examples of program code, we recommend releasing these examples in parallel under your choice of free software license, such as the GNU General Public License, to permit their use in free software.

Appendix D Free Software and Free Manuals

By Richard M. Stallman

The biggest deficiency in free operating systems is not in the software—it is the lack of good free manuals that we can include in these systems. Many of our most important programs do not come with full manuals. Documentation is an essential part of any software package; when an important free software package does not come with a free manual, that is a major gap. We have many such gaps today.

Once upon a time, many years ago, I thought I would learn Perl. I got a copy of a free manual, but I found it hard to read. When I asked Perl users about alternatives, they told me that there were better introductory manuals—but those were not free.

Why was this? The authors of the good manuals had written them for O'Reilly Associates, which published them with restrictive terms—no copying, no modification, source files not available—which exclude them from the free software community.

That wasn't the first time this sort of thing has happened, and (to our community's great loss) it was far from the last. Proprietary manual publishers have enticed a great many authors to restrict their manuals since then. Many times I have heard a GNU user eagerly tell me about a manual that he is writing, with which he expects to help the GNU project—and then had my hopes dashed, as he proceeded to explain that he had signed a contract with a publisher that would restrict it so that we cannot use it.

Given that writing good English is a rare skill among programmers, we can ill afford to lose manuals this way.

Free documentation, like free software, is a matter of freedom, not price. The problem with these manuals was not that O'Reilly Associates charged a price for printed copies–that in itself is fine. The Free Software Foundation http://www.fsf.org/, also sells printed copies of freely distributable manuals at http://www.gnupress.org. However, GNU manuals are available in source code form as well as in paper. GNU manuals come with permission to copy and modify; the Perl manuals do not. These restrictions are the problems.

The criterion for a free manual is pretty much the same as for free software: it is a matter of giving all users certain freedoms. Redistribution (including commercial redistribution) must be permitted, so that the manual can accompany every copy of the program, on-line or on paper. Permission for modification is crucial too.

As a general rule, I don't believe that it is essential for people to have permission to modify all sorts of articles and books. The issues for writings are not necessarily the same as those for software. For example, I don't think you or I are obliged to give permission to modify articles like this one, which describe our actions and our views.

But there is a particular reason why the freedom to modify is crucial for documentation for free software. When people exercise their right to modify the software, and add or change its features, if they are conscientious they will change the manual too—so they can provide accurate and usable documentation with the modified program. A manual which forbids programmers to be conscientious and finish the job, or more precisely requires them to write a new manual from scratch if they change the program, does not fill our community's needs.

While a blanket prohibition on modification is unacceptable, some kinds of limits on the method of modification pose no problem. For example, requirements to preserve the original author's copyright notice, the distribution terms, or the list of authors, are ok. It is also no problem to require modified versions to include notice that they were modified, even to have entire sections that may not be deleted or changed, as long as these sections deal with nontechnical topics. (Some GNU manuals have them.)

These kinds of restrictions are not a problem because, as a practical matter, they don't stop the conscientious programmer from adapting the manual to fit the modified program. In other words, they don't block the free software community from making full use of the manual.

However, it must be possible to modify all the technical content of the manual, and then distribute the result in all the usual media, through all the usual channels; otherwise, the restrictions do block the community, the manual is not free, and so we need another manual.

Unfortunately, it is often hard to find someone to write another manual when a proprietary manual exists. The obstacle is that many users think that a proprietary manual is good enough—so they don't see the need to write a free manual. They do not see that the free operating system has a gap that needs filling.

Why do users think that proprietary manuals are good enough? Some have not considered the issue. I hope this article will do something to change that.

Other users consider proprietary manuals acceptable for the same reason so many people consider proprietary software acceptable: they judge in purely practical terms, not using freedom as a criterion. These people are entitled to their opinions, but since those opinions spring from values which do not include freedom, they are no guide for those of us who do value freedom.

Please spread the word about this issue. We continue to lose manuals to proprietary publishing. If we spread the word that proprietary manuals are not sufficient, perhaps the next person who wants to help GNU by writing documentation will realize, before it is too late, that he must above all make it free.

We can also encourage commercial publishers to sell free, copylefted manuals instead of proprietary ones. One way you can help this is to check the distribution terms of a manual before you buy it, and prefer copylefted manuals to non-copylefted ones.

Index